THE KRONSTADT REBELLION

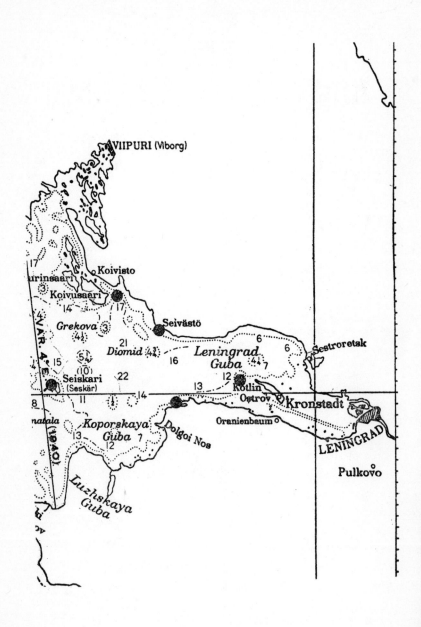

THE
KRONSTADT REBELLION

(The First Armed Revolt Against the Soviets)

by **EMANUEL POLLACK**

PHILOSOPHICAL LIBRARY

New York

CONTENTS

INTRODUCTION

Is a revolt of the Russian people against the Soviet regime possible?

Many people have asked that question.

The answer is: under certain circumstances.

Did the Russian people ever try to rid themselves of their rulers who, by promise of bread, land and peace, tied them to the Communist chariot of world conquest through world revolution?

The answer is: they tried.

It happened in March, 1921. This is the story of the *first armed revolt of the people of Russia against the Soviet rulers,* when the latter were not as strong as they are today; when the Red Army was taking its first steps on the road to power; when the secret police, known then as Cheka, although not as efficient as the NKVD or MGB is now, was no less bloodthirsty.

This is a page from the cruel history of Soviet Russia; it is worth knowing and studying by layman and specialist alike. This page from recent history casts instructive light on the brutal methods of Soviet rulers—whether they be Lenin, Trotsky or Stalin; or Malenkov, Bulganin or Khrushchev.

This is the story of the Kronstadt Rebellion. It is the tragic and heroic tale of the sailors and workers in Kronstadt, a fortress city situated on the island of Kotlin, in the gulf of Finland, 20 miles west of Leningrad.

The Kronstadt Rebellion was the first and last openly organized political opposition of any consequence by the Russian people against the rulers of Soviet Russia.

How did it come about?

Between 1917 and 1921 the Bolsheviks had suppressed numerous minor revolts and mutinies. But the Kronstadt Rebellion stands out in history because of its organization, because of its implications, because it represented the first and last significant internal threat to the existence of the Communist regime, and because the rebels had been loyal Communists.

Trotsky, second in importance only to Lenin at that time, had described the Kronstadt sailors as the "Pride of the Revolution." In 1917, they had enabled him and his comrades to reach the pinnacle of power. Later, he reviled them as traitors and counter-revolutionists and threatened to shoot them "like partridges," and he kept his promise.

The Kronstadters rebelled against the dictatorship of the Communist Party, its monopoly over the life of the people, its absolute rule. In their innocence and ignorance of the real aims and purposes of the Communist Party (although most of them belonged to it), they presumed that the Soviets would be representative bodies of all the people, whether communist, socialist, anarchist or non-party. In their naivete, the sailors demanded freedom of speech, assembly and press. They paid for their naivete with death and exile.

The recent merciless crushing of the Hungarian revolt proved once again that Communists will stop at nothing in order to destroy those who challenge their power. If Americans had been more familiar with the story of the Kronstadt rebellion, they would have been far less surprised at the brutalities following the October, 1956, revolt of the Hungarian people.

In Hungary, as in Kronstadt a third of a century ago, the people asked for an end of the dictatorship of the Communist party. In Hungary, as in Kronstadt, the opposition within the Communist ranks believed the Reds' claim that they represented the working class. The opposition asked for the protection of the rights of labor, for democracy within the Communist Party. In short, they requested the same changes as those once demanded by the sailors and workers of Kronstadt, who also were loyal members of the Party. Later, however, they became fiercely anti-Communist.

As in Lenin's time, the answer in Hungary was the same; bloody suppression. *Power* is the Communists' God. Human sacrifice is the legitimate food of the monster the Communists worship.

THE KRONSTADT REBELLION

FEBRUARY, 1921

At the conclusion of the Civil War—December, 1920—
Soviet Russia was in a state of near collapse.

"She had been devastated from end to end by the
combined destruction of three contending forces—the
Reds, the Whites, and the foreign interventionists—
who had fought along battle lines that had writhed
over a vast part of the nation. The blockade had
throttled that already crumbling economic system.
Peasant opposition to the Government's enforced
policy of food seizure had reduced agriculture to a
level far below national requirements. The whole industrial system, burdened by a cumbersome and un-
workable management scheme, was grinding to a halt.
As a nation Russia had endured, but at a fearful cost
in human suffering.

"Devastation, disorganization, chaos and starva-

tion—such was the legacy which the civil war left to a
nation already bled white by the enormous losses of
the World War."[1]

Now, the weary populace looked forward to relaxation
of the stringent war measures under which they had lived for
years. No longer fighting on all sides—against the Whites
and the foreign interventionists—the people, the plain working people of Russia, who had supported the Bolshevik
regime and fought its battles on many fronts had a legitimate
claim to a respite and a hope for a better life. Instead, the
regime forced the peasant to give up his grain and other
products without compensation, and hungry city folk made
regular trips to the country in search of bread, potatoes, or
anything edible, in exchange for money or the meager pos-
sessions they could spare from their homes or their backs.
What happened to them on their way home from the trips
to the country, full of pain and anxiety, is aptly described
by one who lived in Russia during that period:

"Apropos of the opportunities of bringing something from the country, a whole book could be written on that alone. With the prohibition of trading
came the 'Zagraditelny otryad,' the detachment of soldiers—Chekists at every station to confiscate everything brought by private persons to the city. The
wretched people, after untold difficulties of obtaining
a pass for travel, after days and weeks of exposure at
the stations, or on the roofs and platforms, would bring
a pood [equivalent of 36 English pounds] of flour or
potatoes, only to have it snatched from them by the
otryad.

"In most cases the confiscated stuff was divided by
the defenders of the Communist State among them-

selves. The victims were fortunate indeed if they escaped further trouble. After they were robbed of their precious pack, they were often thrown into gaol for 'speculation.'

"The number of real speculators apprehended was insignificant in comparison with the mass of unfortunate humanity that filled the prisons of Russia for trying to keep from starving to death."[2]

Forced food collections ("Razvyorstka") were one of the features of the post Civil War period. The Bolsheviki claimed that they were compelled to resort to these drastic measures because the peasants refused to feed the cities voluntarily. While priding themselves on being materialists and realists, the Communists seemingly forgot that the matter of feeding the city population was subject to the economic law of exchange. The peasant would part with his products only upon receiving the things he needed. From time immemorial, he had brought his products to the city and traded them for the supplies he wanted. It was not a matter of charity or benevolence. But the promised manufactured goods rarely reached the peasants—when they did arrive, they were frequently damaged, or of incorrect size, or faulty in other ways.

The peasants yearned for a return to the ancient custom of selling their wares directly to the consumers at the old market-place, where they could see and feel and touch the things they needed, and either purchase outright or exchange them for other products. This the Bolsheviks denied them. The government agents who appeared in the villages offered them very little for the yield of their farms, and the peasants could not or would not rely on promises. They refused to turn over their produce to the Government agents.

In answer, the Bolsheviki instituted the Razvyorstka

policy (enforced grain collection), which antagonized the peasantry even further.

In no small degree the Razvyorstka was responsible for the famine of 1921-22. Not only were the peasants robbed of their last pood of flour by Government agents, but very often even the seeds for their next planting were withheld (or taken from them). And when the peasant resisted the Government's attempts to requisition his produce, punitive expeditions were dispatched to the villages. After carting off all the peasants' belongings that they could lay hands on, the troops destroyed the villages as counter-revolutionary nests. This was war. Consequently, if the peasant was not counter-revolutionary previously, the Razvyortska, the punitive expeditions, the general lawlessness of the bureaucracy made him so. Now the countryside became permeated with the counter-revolutionary spirit, but fear and resignation kept the peasants from open revolt. Nevertheless, their passive resistance so endangered the Communist regime that it eventually brought about an entire change in the nation's taxation and trade policies.

Another evil of that period was conscript labor. The Communists called it mobilization of labor and looked upon it as a tremendous achievement. Parasites would not be tolerated—everyone must work in the land of socialism. In the greatest capitalist country, the United States, almost everybody works too, even those who exploit the labor of others. If the latter element was eliminated in Russia right after the October Revolution, presumably the rest of the people—worker, peasant, office employee, manager—were busy in their regular occupations. Left to himself, each man or woman would discover for himself the type of work he wanted to do and what he was best fitted for. This natural adjustment would have placed each person in his proper place of occupation. But the Bolsheviks could not let nature take its course; otherwise there would have been no justification for the state to control every human activity. Conscription of labor in Russia meant a temporary reversion to chattel slavery and the exchange of bourgeois parasitism for the parasitism and deadweight of the Bolshevik machine.

In spite of everything else, those were the golden days of a worker's freedom in his factory or shop. He still considered himself master in his house; he still was under the illusion that the factory belonged to the workers—an illusion of which he was soon to be cured.

Labor conscription, however, failed to increase worker output, since the "parasites" who were driven to labor by force were, of course, middle class people, former government employees, storekeepers, members of the intelligentsia, the so-called "declassed elements" who never had done physical work before. Indiscriminately, they were assigned to the heaviest sort of manual labor—chopping wood, shoveling snow, cutting ice—with the result that the aged and thinly clad conscripts fell ill with respiratory and lung infections. Only after a mass breakdown in health did the government create a special bureau to match the work to the individual's physical fitness.

Through the years of the civil war and afterward, Russia was in the grip of the red terror, led by the dreaded Cheka. Now, during the first months of 1921, the secret police found more justification than ever for its work. The general discontent was greater, outbreaks of mutinies and uprisings sprang up more frequently. *For the Bolshevik rulers, the situation became one of self-defense against the population.* Indiscriminate jailing and killing of people, torture and terror increased mercilessly.

There exist today a few books on this subject written by Russians in the early twenties; they preserve for posterity some of the most terrible pages of Russian history. Among them is "Red Terror in Russia," by the writer and historian S. P. Melgunov, published in Berlin in 1924. It seems to be the only systematized record of the crimes committed by the "Sword of the Revolution," the Cheka. In the foreword, S. P. Melgunov writes:

"I wish that those who take this book into their hands will have the courage to read it through. . . . Indeed, it requires iron nerves in order to live through and assimilate the horrors which are presented in the following pages.

"Historians have in the past and try now to explain and even find justification for the period of terror of the French Revolution. . . . I do not wish to explain a phenomenon, which can only be branded by public morality in its past as in the present. I only wish to re-create the picture of that past and of the present. Let sociologist and moralist seek explanations of the contemporary human brutalities in the legacy of the past and in the bloody vapors of the last European war, in the decline of human morality, in the distortion of the bases of human psyche and reasoning. Let the neurologists relegate it to the sick phenomena of the age. . . .

"My desire is only to re-create a realistic picture of the past and present which is so distorted under the hand of the historical researchers and in the subjective examinations by the contemporary practical politician."

In the Crimea, in the Kuban region, in Georgia, in the Ukraine—wherever a semblance of resistance to or dissatisfaction with the red rule appeared—the opponents of the regime were drowned in rivers of blood.

Because of space limitations and because our essay is confined to the Kronstadt Rebellion and the events immediately leading to it, it is impossible to include in these pages a detailed account of the crimes and brutalities committed in each section of Russia during and after the civil war. For the sake of illustrations, however, we shall quote a bit more from S. P. Melgunov's catalogue of crimes in "The Red Terror in Russia":

" 'Posledniye Novosti' (Prof. Miliukov's newspaper published in Paris) of May 5th publishes the following figures about the activities of the Cheka for the first three months of the new year (1921). The newspaper writes that it obtained its facts from an official report: shot—4,300 men; suppressed—114 rebellions. This refers to acts committed in 12 central regions (gubernias) of Russia proper. Mass executions were carried out in Yaroslavl, Saratov, Samara, Kazan and Kursk. During January, in Moscow alone, 347 persons were executed. According to reports of the newspaper 'Golos Rossyi' (Voice of Russia), which obtained its information from the statistical department of the Commissariat of Railroad Communications, in 1921, 1,759 passengers and employees were shot by the decision of the railroad tribunals. The newspaper 'Revolutsionnaya Rossia' No. 12-13 reports that when six men escaped from the concentration camp in Yekaterinburg, the overseer Uranov lined up all the White officers in the camp. He selected twenty-five at random and ordered them shot as a lesson for the other inmates.

"The 'uprising' of railroad workers at Yekaterino-slav resulted in 51 victims. Possibly more. Z. U. Arbatov, in his memoirs 'Yekaterinoslav in 1917-1922' bears witness to the fact that 200 workers were arrested in connection with the above mentioned 'revolt.' Fifty-one of them were sentenced to be shot immediately.

Arbatov writes:

'During the night of June 2nd, those sentenced to death were brought in two trucks to a steep shore of the river Dnieper, a machine gun at their backs. Many of the slain victims fell straight into the river. The swift current carried away the dead bodies. Other bodies remained on the shore.'

"The remaining sentenced railroad workers were sent for disposition to the All-Ukrainian Cheka in Kharkov. Thus, according to the Bolsheviks themselves, the 'Little Kronstadt' was suppressed.

"The 'conspiracy' in Byisk resulted in 300 arrested and 18 shot; the 'conspiracy' in the Semirechensk region resulted in the execution of 148 officers and kulaks. The 'conspiracy' in Yelisavetgrad (in December) brought 85 arrested, 55 shot. And so forth, and so forth, without end. . . ."[3]

Such was the state of affairs in Russia at large. In some respects, Petrograd, the city which set the pace and example for the rest of the country, was in an even worse condition. Its population was the first to bear the brunt of every new Bolshevik experiment.

In February—the month of greatest pertinence to the subject of our essay—Petrograd was cold and hungry and bitterly disappointed. The workers who had fought for the Revolution, who had made possible the existence of the Soviet power, were hungry and neglected. Finally, on the 24th of February, to gain their modest demands, the workers went on strike.

The strike began at the Troubetskoy factory. What did the workers demand? That their food rations be increased, as promised long ago, and that they be given shoes. They knew that party members in the shops had been provided with shoes and clothing. Were they (the strikers) considered second-rate citizens by the government? The meeting called by the workers to discuss ways of improving the situation had been forbidden by the authorities. The Soviet of Petrograd had refused to enter into any discussions until the men returned to their jobs. At each factory excited workers gathered to talk over their problems. In the old czarist manner, the authorities sent armed "kursanti" (the cadets of the military schools) to disperse the workers, who quickly submitted. They had no arms to resist, even if they were in the mood to do so. Word of the treatment of the Troubetskoy workers spread to other factories. Out of protest and a feeling of solidarity, the workers of the Admiralty shops, the Patronny mills, the Baltiysky and Lafern factories streamed into the streets of Petrograd in demonstration. Immediately the authorities dispatched soldiers to break up the demonstrations. The workers could not believe that Red Army men would ride rough-shod over the working people—but they did.

Inevitably, to the economic demands such as provision of food and fuel were added political demands. The arbitrariness and ruthless acts of the government, the application of the fist and butt-end of guns to the backs of protesting workers had immediate repercussions: unsigned declarations appeared on the walls of the city, demanding "a complete change in the policies of the Government," and freedom to control their own destinies. With each passing day, as the tension mounted, new and more insistent demands were pasted on walls and buildings. Finally, a call appeared for convening the Constituent Assembly. Thereupon the authorities declared martial law. They ordered the workers to return to their factories on the threat of depriving them entirely of their rations. When the threats failed, the Bolsheviki liquidated a number of unions and arrested their officials and the more recalcitrant workers.

In a capitalist, democratic country, the strike is a mighty weapon. Strikers have recourse to the general public, whose sympathies they seek and often find. Not so in a totalitarian state, where all economic means, including the distribution of food, clothing, fuel, etc., are rigidly controlled by the state. If necessary, the Bolsheviks were determined to starve the striking Petrograd workers into submission. And there was no way to stop them. Help from the public? The population itself was in desperate need of food and fuel. Any attempt of outsiders to aid the strikers, even if the outsiders were neighbors, was considered an act of sabotage by the authorities. The strikers were doomed from the start.

Emma Goldman,* who witnessed this significant upheaval of the Petrograd workers in the fateful days of February, 1921, relates in her autobiography an interesting conversation she had at that time with a Bolshevik official regarding strike possibilities in Soviet Russia and their meaning:

" 'Strikes under the dictatorship of the proletariat!' the official exclaimed. 'There is no such thing.'

"Against whom, indeed, should the workers strike in Soviet Russia, he had argued. Against themselves? They were the masters of the country, politically as well as industrially. To be sure, there were some among the toilers who were not yet fully class-con-

---

* Emma Goldman (1869-1940). Famous Russian-born American anarchist. Active in the American labor-movement. In 1919 deported to Russia but left that country in 1921. Wrote My Disillusionment in Russia (1923), Social Significance of Modern Drama (1914), autobiography Living My Life (1931).

scious and aware of their own true interests. These were sometimes disgruntled, but they were elements incited by the shkurniki (self-seekers) and enemies of the Revolution. Skinners, parasites, they were, who were purposely misleading the ignorant people. They were the worst kind of sabotazhniki, no better than out-and-out counter-revolutionists, and of course the Soviet authorities had to protect the country against their kind. Most of them were in prison."[4]

Theoretically, the Bolsheviki had a valid argument. Against whom did the workers strike? Against their own workers' government? Against themselves, against their own interests? Hardly. The fiction of the identification of the Soviet Government with the interests of the workers had long been exploded. The two parties have much less in common than the employer and his employees in a capitalist country. As early as 1921, the Petrograd workers recognized the fiction. They struck, not against themselves, but against a force which had usurped their power, against a force which spoke to the world in their name, and to this day continues to do so.

The Bolsheviks recognized that the Petrograd workers and their allies, the Kronstadt sailors, must be taught an everlasting lesson if the Bolsheviks were to survive as a dictatorial party. Herein lies the reason for the government brutality in the strike-breaking activities and the consequent blood-letting in Kronstadt.

* * *

Disturbed by the events in Petrograd and puzzled by the Government's actions, the Kronstadt sailors, who were considered the elite of the Revolution, decided to learn the true situation for themselves, without the help of government

agents. Quietly they sent an investigating committee to the
area. The committee's report provoked deep indignation
among the sailors at the treatment of their brothers, the
workers. Thereupon, while remaining loyal and devoted to
the Revolution, the Communist Party, and the Soviets, the
sailors (from the warships *Sevastopol* and *Petropavlovsk*)
adopted a resolution which condemned the arbitrariness of
certain officials and demanded greater freedom for labor and
peasant groups and the release of labor and political prisoners.

The sailors' attitude caused elation among Petrograd's
workers. Helpless and defenseless against the power of the
state which they themselves had created, they were over-
joyed at the sudden helping hand outstretched to them from
the fortress-city. There was real hope now that a just settlement would be forthcoming.

Then on March 1st, a huge open-air rally was organized
in Kronstadt, attended by sixteen thousand sailors, Red Army-
men, and workers. At this meeting, the First and Second
Squadrons of the Baltic Fleet stationed at Kronstadt followed
the example of the sailors of *Petropavlovsk* and *Sevastopol.*
With only three dissenting votes—those of the chairman of
the mass meeting, Vassiliev, President of the Kronstadt
Soviet; Kuzmin, Commissar of the Baltic Fleet; and Kalinin,
President of the All-Russian Soviet Executive Committee—resolutions favoring the workers' demands were adopted. Could
anything demonstrate more clearly the unity and solidarity
prevalent at the gathering?

Was the meeting portentous of a forthcoming revolt
against the Soviets? Not at all. The resolutions were strongly
Sovietist, the assembly indicated no opposition to the Communists, and the rally itself was under the auspices of the
Kronstadt Soviet. Despite his opposition to their demands,
the sailors escorted Kalinin to and from the railroad station
with friendliness and respect.

In order that the reader himself may judge the true character of the demands of the Kronstadt sailors, we reproduce the document in full:

*Resolution of the General Meeting of
the Crews of the First and Second Squadrons
of the Baltic Fleet. March 1, 1921.*

"Having heard the Report of the Representatives sent by the General Meeting of Ship Crews to Petrograd to investigate the situation there, Resolved:

1. In view of the fact that the present Soviets do not express the will of the workers and the peasants, immediately to hold new elections by secret ballot, the preelection campaign to have full freedom of agitation among the workers and peasants;
2. To establish freedom of speech and press for workers and peasants, for Anarchists and left Socialist parties;
3. To secure freedom of assembly for labor unions and peasant organizations;
4. To call a non-partisan Conference of the workers, Red Army soldiers and sailors of Petrograd, Kronstadt, and Petrograd Province, no later than March 10, 1921;
5. To liberate all political prisoners of Socialist parties, as well as all workers, peasants, soldiers and sailors imprisoned in connection with the labor and peasant movements;
6. To elect a Commission to review the cases of those held in prisons and concentration camps;
7. To abolish all politotdeli (political bureaus) because no party should be given special privileges in the propagation of its ideas or receive the

financial support of the Government for such purposes. Instead, there should be established educational and cultural commissions, locally elected and financed by the Government;

8. To abolish immediately all zagraditelniye otriadi (armed units organized by the Bolsheviki for the purpose of suppressing traffic and confiscating foodstuffs);

9. To equalize the rations of all who work, with the exception of those employed in trades detrimental to health;

10. To abolish the Communist fighting detachments in all branches of the Army, as well as the Communist guards kept on duty in mills and factories. Should such guards or military detachments be found necessary, they are to be appointed in the Army from the ranks, and in the factories according to the judgment of the workers;

11. To give the peasants full freedom of action in regard to their land, and also the right to keep cattle, on condition that the peasants manage with their own means; that is, without employing hired labor;

12. To request all branches of the Army, as well as our comrades, the military kursanti, to concur in our resolutions;

14. To appoint a Travelling Commission of Control;

15. To permit free kustarnoye (individual small scale) production by one's own efforts.

Resolution passed unanimously by Brigade Meeting, two persons refraining from voting;

PETRICHENKO
Chairman Brigade Meeting

PEREPELKIN
Secretary

Resolution passed by an overwhelming majority of the Kronstadt garrison.

VASSILIEV
Chairman

Together with comrade Kalinin, Vassiliev votes against the Resolution."[5]

Note that the Kronstadters did not issue a call for the Constituent Assembly, although in Petrograd there was a decided trend in that direction. They still believed in and supported the Soviets.

Just as these demands were, they could never be accepted by the ruling Bolsheviks. They were a clear expression of the desires of the sailors, soldiers and workers of Kronstadt for democracy, for genuine self-rule, public and social control of functionaries, the civilian over military, a wider representation in the Soviets, and the abolition of arbitrariness of the special Communist organizations. Finally, they represented a demand that the Communist Party share its power with other Socialist parties. These demands were essentially anti-Communist.

The Bolsheviki quickly realized that these fifteen points meant more than a petition for the rectification of their attitudes toward the economic needs of the Petrograd workers. They were a demand for the return of the rights and privileges of the working class. From the Communists' point of view, the Kronstadt sailors and workers were rebels against the regime and its power. Such temerity was unforgivable. Also unforgivable was the impropriety of calling officials publicly to order, of divulging that the prisons and concentration camps were filled with workers, peasants and soldiers, of revealing that the workers' land was ruled by a

brutal police force—at a time when Trotsky and his comrades were heralding the establishment of a workers' paradise.
To the Bolsheviks these were unforgivable crimes punishable
by death.

Who were they who called the rulers to order? Only the
people who had given of their strength and hopes in the Revolution, thus affording these officials the opportunity to become the chosen ones of the first workers' state. Is it any won-
der, then, that the peasant-president, Kalinin, the Commissar
of the Baltic Fleet, Kuzmin, and the President of the Kronstadt Soviet, Vassiliev, called the sailors "traitors," the Petrograd workers "skurniki" (skinners), and all of them "counter-
revolutionists"?

*   *   *

At the mass-meeting on March 1st, three hundred delegates were elected as a permanent body to represent the fleet,
the garrison and the trade-unions of Kronstadt in negotiations
with the Communist authorities. At a later meeting, when
they learned that Commissar Kuzmin had ordered the re-
moval of all food (and munitions) from Kronstadt—dooming
the city to starvation—the delegates had Kuzmin and Vassiliev arrested, thus forestalling the spiriting away of their
supplies. Detaining the Soviet representatives could not be
construed as a rebellious act, since Communist delegates attended the meeting and had an equal voice in the delibera-
tions and decisions of the meeting. This constituted another
proof that, in spite of their severe criticism, the Kronstadters
retained their confidence in the Soviet regime. Indeed, they
selected a committee of thirty men to confer with the Petrograd Soviet in order to reach an amicable settlement of the
strike.

Nevertheless, as indicated above, the authorities probed

more deeply into the situation. They recognized that the fifteen-point resolution of the Kronstadt garrison was directed at the very vitals of the newly established Soviet regime, which demanded blind obedience from the populace. It could not be dismissed as a simple proposal drawn up by honest, naive sailors who were disturbed by the unjust treatment of the Petrograd workers. As leading Bolsheviks immediately understood, the Kronstadt sailors were striking at the dominance of the Communist party in Russia to the exclusion of any other. Since a communist dictatorship was one of the basic tenets of Bolshevik philosophy, the effectiveness of the Kronstadt garrison as a nest of constant dissatisfaction had to be destroyed. The long sought pretext to liquidate the "flower of the Revolution"—which had become much more than a nuisance with its constant reminders to the leading Bolsheviks of the pristine purity of the Revolution's original aims—was now at hand.

Within a few hours after the Kronstadt mass-meeting, all Petrograd learned of a special communique signed by Lenin and Trotsky, charging that Kronstadt had mutinied against the Soviet Government. The statement denounced the sailors as "tools of former tsarist generals who together with Socialist-Revolutionary* traitors staged a counter-revolutionary conspiracy against the proletarian Republic."[6] Immediately, the Communist press opened a campaign of calumny and vituperation against the Kronstadt sailors and soldiers; they were accused of having joined the ranks of the counter-revolutionary White Guards headed by the "Tsarist General Kozlovsky."

---

* Socialist Revolutionary Party first appeared on the scene in Russia in 1902. Fully organized in 1905. The S.R.'s, as they were called to distinguish them from the S.D.'s (members of the Social-Democratic Party) concentrated their attention not on the workmen but on the peasantry. The Bolsheviks considered the S.R. Party a petty-bourgeois party. It was persecuted and finally liquidated by the Soviets.

No one dared raise the question of how any White Guards were able to exist in Kronstadt under the Cheka's unceasing vigil. And who was General Kozlovsky? How had he survived all the revolutionary years since 1917?

Of course there were no White Guards in Kronstadt; they were a pure invention of the ruling Bolsheviks. There was a General Kozlovsky, however, an old and feeble man, without following or influence, and he had been placed in Kronstadt as an artillery specialist by Trotsky himself. The Bolsheviks dubbed Kozlovsky the leader of the "counter-revolution" only because they needed a scapegoat and a name. Unfortunately, the Kronstadt sailors, outlawed and cut off from the rest of Russia, could not disprove the lie, and it served the Communist rulers of Petrograd well as a means of inciting their followers against Kronstadt.

II

THE PETROGRAD SOVIET IN SESSION

On March 4th the Petrograd Soviet held a meeting to decide the fate of Kronstadt.

Many people believed that the assembly would provide the atmosphere needed for calm deliberation and the opportunity for other than the official view of the situation to be presented and discussed. However, the hysteria pervading official circles and the howling of the press, on instigation from the same quarters, were ominous danger signals. Zinoviev, President of the Petrograd Soviet, and Chairman of the specially created Committee of Defense, was thrown into panic at the first sign of discontent among the workers. He lost his head completely when he learned that the local garrison had expressed sympathy with the strikers. Thereupon, he ordered a machine-gun for his protection placed at his residence, and bombarded Moscow with wild stories about the threat to Soviet power in Petrograd.

The Tauride Palace, where the assembly gathered, was

an armed camp. A special body of kursanti surrounded the platform and Chekist soldiers with fixed bayonets stood between the platform and the audience. Zinoviev presided. He was exceedingly nervous. Several times he rose to speak and then sat down again. When he finally took the floor, he kept jerking his head right and left, as if fearing sudden attack. In a shrill voice, he castigated the phantom general Kozlovsky, who allegedly had instigated the Kronstadt rebellion, and his tsarist aides. Then it was old Kalinin's turn to harangue the Kronstadters, who only a few days before had greeted him with song and music.

"No measure can be too severe for the counter-revolutionists who dare to raise their hand against our glorious Revolution,"[7] he declared.

Other speakers followed the lead of Zinoviev and Kalinin and denounced the Kronstadt sailors in the worst terms, calling for the blood of their former brothers in arms, the acclaimed heroes of the Revolution, arousing those in the audience ignorant of the facts to a frenzy of hatred and revenge.

When the meeting was thrown open for floor discussion, a workingman from the Petrograd Arsenal sitting in the front row demanded to be heard. Ignoring the constant interruptions, he declared that, as a delegate of the Arsenal's workers, he protested the misrepresentations uttered from the platform against the brave and loyal men of Kronstadt; that the workers were forced to strike because of the Government's indifference to their complaints; that the Kronstadt sailors, far from being counter-revolutionists, were devoted to the Revolution heart and soul.

Here is an eye-witness report of the scene that followed:

"Facing Zinoviev and pointing his finger directly at him, the worker in a moving voice said:

" 'It's the cruel indifference of yourself and of your party that drove us to strike and that roused the sympathy of our brother sailors, who had fought side by side with us in the Revolution. They are guilty of no crime, and you know it. Consciously you malign them and call for their destruction.'

"Cries of 'Counter-revolutionist! Traitor! Skurnik! Menshevik bandit!' turned the assembly into a bedlam. The old worker remained standing, his voice rising above the tumult.

" 'Barely three years ago Lenin, Trotsky, Zinoviev, and all of you,' he shouted, 'were denounced as traitors and German spies. We, the workers and sailors, had come to your rescue and saved you from the Kerensky Government. It was we who placed you in power. Have you forgotten that? Now you threaten us with the sword. Remember you are playing with fire. You are repeating the blunders and crimes of the Kerensky Government. Beware that a similar fate does not overtake you!'

"The challenge made Zinoviev wince. The others on the platform moved uneasily in their seats. The Communist audience seemed awed for an instant by the portentous warning, and in that moment there rang out another voice. A tall man in a sailor's uniform stood up in the back. Nothing had changed in the revolutionary spirit of his brother of the sea, he declared. To the last man they were ready to defend the Revolution with their every drop of blood. Then he proceeded to read the Kronstadt resolution adopted at the mass meeting on March 1st. The uproar his daring evoked made it impossible for any but those nearest to hear him. But he stood his ground and kept on reading to the end.

"The only reply to these two sturdy sons of the Revolution was Zinoviev's resolution demanding the complete and immediate surrender of Kronstadt on pain of extermination. It was rushed through the session amidst a pandemonium of confusion, with every opposing voice gagged."[8]

Those who usurp power use any and every means to maintain it. Political trickery of the kind employed by Zinoviev and his comrades to frame the Kronstadt sailors was one method. It served the immediate needs of the despotic power in the saddle. The enormous lie of the Kronstadt plot had weathered its first big trial. Those that followed were much easier to perpetrate.

III

WITHIN THE CITY OF KRONSTADT

Perhaps it would be helpful to review the fast breaking developments leading to the Kronstadt Rebellion.

On February 28, the crew of the warship *Petropavlovsk* passed a resolution, later concurred in by the sailors of the warship *Sevastopol,* in which they demanded, among other things, free elections to the Kronstadt Soviet, whose term of office was about to expire. They also sent a committee to Petrograd to ascertain the facts about the strike movement.

On March 1st, the Kronstadt sailors, soldiers and workers gathered, 16,000 strong, on the Yakorny Square to hear the report of the committee. The rally was presided over by the Communist Vassiliev, Chairman of the Executive Committee of the Kronstadt Soviet. Also attending were Kalinin, President of the All-Russian Soviet Executive Committee, and Kuzmin, the Commissar of the Baltic Fleet.

The Sailors' Committee, sent to investigate the unrest in

Petrograd, delivered its report, which verified the miserable conditions of the workers. The audience openly expressed its indignation at the contempt shown by the Communists toward the workers' demands and the methods they used to crush all protests. Thereupon, the resolution passed by the *Petropavlovsk* sailors was presented to the meeting for approval. President Kalinin and Commissar Kuzmin took the floor to attack the resolution, the Petrograd workers, as well as the Kronstadt sailors. They failed to convince the audience, however, and the *Petropavlovsk* resolution was passed with but three dissenting votes.

Then it was agreed to dispatch a delegation of Kronstadters to Petrograd to explain the Kronstadt demands to the workers and soldiers there and to request that delegates be sent to the fortress city to learn for themselves what Kronstadt's attitude really was. Upon arrival in Petrograd, the Committee of thirty representatives from Kronstadt was arrested by the Communists, and their fate remains unknown to this day.

Another decision reached at the rally was to call a conference of delegates for March 2nd to discuss election methods to fill the seats of the expiring local Soviet.

Again, we must emphasize that the conference had no thought of insurrection. Nothing in their behaviour could be interpreted as rebellious. They had their grievances, they considered it important to air them; they had their demands which they felt were entirely in the spirit of the Revolution and they sought the means to satisfy them. The Kronstadt sailors were the staunchest supporters of the Soviet system, but they were opposed to the dictatorship of any political party. They wanted the Soviets to reflect the true needs and will of the workers and peasants.

On March 2nd, 300 delegates from the garrison and city of Kronstadt met in the House of Education, formerly the

School of Engineering. The first speaker was Kuzmin, the Commissar of the Baltic Fleet. He incensed the audience with his arrogance and insolence. He denied the labor disorders in Petrograd, declaring that the city was quiet and the workers satisfied. He praised the work of the Commissars, questioned Kronstadt's revolutionary motives, made unworthy insinuations, and threatened the gathering with dire consequences.

"If you want open warfare," Kuzmin concluded, "you shall have it, for the Communists will not give up the reins of government. We will fight to the bitter end."[9]

Vassiliev, Chairman of the Kronstadt Soviet, was the next speaker and he ranted in the same vein. After these two tirades, the delegates could no longer hope to reach an understanding with the Government representatives.

As stated by Izvestia, of the Provisional Revolutionary Committee of Kronstadt, No. 9, March 11, 1921:

> "It was apparent that we could not trust comrades Kuzmin and Vassiliev any more, and that it was necessary to detain them temporarily, especially because the Communists were in possession of arms, and we had no access to the telephones. The soldiers stood in fear of the Commissars . . . and the Communists did not permit gatherings of the garrison to take place."[10]

Kuzmin and Vassiliev were arrested. However, the motion to detain other Communists present at the meeting was voted down because the delegates held that rank and file Communists must be considered on an equal footing with representatives of other organizations and accorded the same rights and treatment. (While distinguishing between the rulers and those ruled, they still hoped to work out an agreement with the Communist Party and the Bolshevik

Government.) Then the conference discussed possible methods of defending Kronstadt against Bolshevik attack, which they knew was imminent. The Presidium of the Conference was turned into a Provisional Revolutionary Committee, charged with the duty of preserving order and safety in the city, and making the necessary preparations for holding new elections to the Kronstadt Soviet.

On the same day, March 2nd, the Soviet Government issued a statement signed by Lenin and Trotsky, which denounced the Kronstadt movement as a mutiny against the Communist authorities. The sailors were charged with being the "tools of the former Tsarist generals who, together with Socialist-Revolutionary traitors, staged a counter-revolutionary conspiracy against the proletarian Republic." The Kronstadt movement for free Soviets was characterized as "the work of Entente interventionists and French spies."

"On February 28," the statement read, "there were passed by the men of the *Petropavlovsk* resolutions breathing the spirit of the Black Hundreds. Then there appeared on the scene the group of the former general Kozlovsky. He and three of his officers, whose names we have not yet ascertained, have openly assumed the role of rebellion. Thus the meaning of recent events has become evident. Behind the Socialist-Revolutionaries again stands a Tsarist general. In view of all this the Council of Labor and Defense orders:

1. To declare the former general Kozlovsky and his aides outlawed;
2. To put the city of Petrograd and the Petrograd Province under martial law;
3. To place supreme power over the whole Petrograd District into the hands of the Petrograd Committee of Defense."[11]

As noted earlier, there was indeed a former general, Kozlovsky, in Kronstadt, and it was Trotsky who had placed him there as an artillery specialist. He played no role whatever in the Kronstadt events, but the Bolsheviki cleverly used his name to slander the sailors as enemies of the Soviet Republic and their movement as counter-revolutionary.

Moscow continued its campaign of misrepresentation. On March 3 the Bolshevik radio sent out the following message to the world:

". . . That armed uprising of the former general Kozlovsky has been organized by the spies of the Entente, like many similar previous plots, is evident from the bourgeois French newspaper, *Matin*, which two weeks prior to the Kozlovsky rebellion published the following telegram from Helsingfors:

" 'As a result of the recent Kronstadt uprising the Bolshevik authorities have taken steps to isolate Kronstadt and to prevent the sailors and soldiers of Kronstadt from entering Petrograd.'

". . . It is clear that the Kronstadt uprising was made in Paris and organized by the French secret service."[12]

Petrograd meanwhile was "cleansed" of all "unreliable" elements, i.e., persons displaying sympathy with the Kronstadt sailors. Many soldiers, workers, and sailors were placed under arrest. Several Army regiments and all Petrograd sailors thought to be "politically untrustworthy" were ordered to distant points, and the families of Kronstadt sailors living in Petrograd were taken into custody as hostages.

On March 4, the Petrograd Committee of Defense informed Kronstadt of its actions by scattering copies of a proclamation from an airplane over the city. The proclamation read:

> "The Committee of Defense declares that the arrested are held as hostages for the Commissar of the Baltic Fleet, N. N. Kuzmin; the Chairman of the Kronstadt Soviet, T. Vassiliev; and other Communists. If the least harm be suffered by our detained comrades, the hostages will pay with their lives."[13]

Kronstadt's reply was:

> "We do not want bloodshed. Not a single Communist has been shot by us."[14]

*   *   *

A curious thing then happened. The Kronstadters were, of course, beset by worries and fears of provoking the authorities, and knew that they must tread cautiously so as not to step on the sensitive toes of the Communist rulers. But a strange exhilaration seized Kronstadt.

> "For the first time since the Communist Party assumed control of the Revolution and the fate of Russia, Kronstadt felt itself free."[15]

A new enthusiasm, reminiscent of the days of October, 1905, when heroism and devotion played such a decisive role, gripped the people.

> "A new spirit of solidarity and brotherhood brought the sailors, the soldiers of the garrison, the factory workers, and the nonpartisan elements to-

gether in united effort for their common cause. Even
Communists were infected by the fraternization of the
whole city and joined in the work preparatory to the
approaching elections to the Kronstadt Soviet."[16]

The first duty of the Provisional Revolutionary Committee of Kronstadt was to maintain order, to prevent skirmishes
from upsetting the city's normal life. The next step they took
was to publish a newspaper, the official organ of the Committee, the Daily Izvestia. In its first issue (No. 1, March 3,
1921), the Committee made the following appeal to the people, so characteristic of the attitude and temper of the sailors:

> "The Revolutionary Committee is most concerned
> that no blood be shed. It has exerted its best efforts
> to organize revolutionary order in the city, the fort-
> ress and the forts. Comrades and citizens, do not
> suspend work! Workers, remain at your machines;
> sailors and soldiers, be at your posts. All Soviet em-
> ployees and institutions should continue their labors.
> The Provisional Revolutionary Committee calls upon
> you, comrades and citizens, to give it your support
> and aid. Its mission is to organize, in fraternal coop-
> eration with you, the conditions necessary for honest
> and just elections to the new Soviet."[17]

From the first issue to the last of this short-lived newspaper, the major theme was that the Revolutionary Committee and the people they represented had one aspiration: free
Soviets, or Councils, as the only road to liberation from the
oppression of Communist bureaucracy. By radio and on the
pages of their newspaper, the Committee, of course, protested indignantly against the Bolshevik campaign of calumny. It appealed to the working people of Russia and

the world for understanding, sympathy and help. On March 6th, the Committee broadcast the following radio message:

"Our cause is just: we stand for the power of Soviets, not parties. We stand for freely elected representatives of the laboring masses. The Soviets manipulated by the Communist Party have always been deaf to our needs and demands; the only reply we have ever received was shooting. . . . Comrades! They not only deceive you: they deliberately pervert the truth and resort to most despicable defamation. . . . In Kronstadt the whole power is exclusively in the hands of the revolutionary sailors, soldiers and workers—not counter-revolutionists led by some Kozlovsky, as the lying Moscow radio tries to make believe. . . . Do not delay, comrades! Join us, get in touch with us: demand admission to Kronstadt for your delegates. . . ."[18]

Not only was there order in the city, but justice prevailed. The Committee established and firmly adhered to the principle of "equal rights for all, privilege to none." Food rations were distributed equitably; special rations and delicacies were reserved for hospitals and children's homes.

There were many members of the Communist Party in Kronstadt. What was their attitude toward the Revolutionary Committee? They were so impressed by the Committee's fair and generous behaviour towards them that they had nothing but respect for it. In spite of the fact that the Petrograd Communists held the sailors' families as hostages, in spite of their repressions, Kronstadt Communists were neither arrested nor molested. The revolutionary fervor and sincerity of the Committee won the hearts of many Communists in

Kronstadt. Many of them condemned the Central Government and endorsed the stand and measures of the Provisional Committee. Many publicly announced their withdrawal from the Party as a protest against its despotism and bureaucratic corruption. Soon resignations from the Kronstadt Communist Party threatened to become a general exodus. (The Executive Committee of the Communist Party of Russia considered its Kronstadt section so "demoralized" after the defeat of the city that it ordered a complete re-registration of all Party members there.)

Numerous civil and military organizations in Kronstadt expressed their opposition to the Moscow regime and their entire agreement with the Kronstadters' demands. Following is a resolution passed by a Red Army unit, characteristic of the new attitude and spirit:

"We, Red Army soldiers of the Fort 'Krasnoarmeetz', stand wholly with the Provisional Revolutionary Committee, and to the very last we will defend the Revolutionary Committee, the workers and the peasants. . . . Let no one believe the lies of the Communist proclamations thrown from airplanes. We have no generals here and no Tsarist officers. Kronstadt has always been the city of workers and peasants, and so it will remain. The generals are in the service of the Communists. . . . At this moment, when the fate of the country is in the balance, we, who have taken the power into our own hands and who have entrusted the Revolutionary Committee with leadership in the fight—we declare to the whole garrison and to the workers that we are prepared to die for the liberty of the laboring masses. Freed from the three-year-old Communist yoke and terror, we shall die rather than recede a single step. Long live Free Russia of the Working People!

> CREW OF THE
> FORT 'KRASNOARMEETZ.' "

Izvestia, No. 5, March 7, 1921."[19]

These were the bitter, challenging words of an enslaved people. For the first time, they raised their voices, demanding to be "freed from the three-year-old Communist yoke and terror." The Krasnoarmeetz soldiers expressed the will of the downtrodden for a new Revolution, the Third Revolution. In the leading editorial of the March 8th Izvestia (No. 6), titled "What We Are Fighting For," we read:

"With the October Revolution the working class had hoped to achieve its emancipation. But there resulted an even greater enslavement of human personality.

"The power of the police and gendarme regime fell into the hands of the usurpers—the Communists—who, instead of giving the people liberty, have instilled in them only the constant fear of Cheka, which by its horrors surpasses even the gendarme regime of Tsarism. . . .

"Worst and most criminal of all is the spiritual cabal of the Communists: they have laid their hand also on the internal world of the laboring masses, compelling everyone to think according to Communist prescription. . . .

"Here is raised the banner of rebellion against the three-year-old tyranny and oppression of Communist autocracy, which has put in the shade the three-hundred-year-old despotism of monarchism. Here, in

Kronstadt, has been laid the cornerstone of the *Third Revolution* which is to break the last chains of the worker and open the new, broad road to Socialist creativeness. . . .

"Without firing a single shot, without shedding a drop of blood, the first step has been taken. Those who labor need no blood. They will shed it only in self-defense. . . ."[20]

Love for a free Russia and confidence in gaining eventual support from the entire nation, particularly Petrograd, had inspired the Kronstadt Izvestia to write this fiery challenge.

But the Kronstadt sailors did not yet realize the depth of Bolshevik vindictiveness, their calculated cruelty toward those who dared question their stranglehold on the government apparatus. The call to arms against the Kronstadt "insurrection" was approaching. The climax was near at hand.

The most curious aspect of the situation was that, regardless of the defiant statements issuing from Kronstadt, the bitter criticism of Communist rule, and the verbal blasts of the Communist authorities, few believed that a physical attack would be launched against the city. Despite the fierce repressive measures, and even after the Bolsheviks ignored all demands for the liberation of hostages held in Petrograd, the Kronstadters were certain that the Government would not raise its hand against them, no matter what the provocation. They could not bring themselves to believe that they, who had made the October Revolution possible, who had put the Bolsheviks into power, would be treated as criminal counter-revolutionists. Since the sailors possessed only peaceful intentions, they believed that the other side, too, would not resort to arms. Kronstadt refused to imitate the Communist example of vengeance and warned the population against unjust treatment of Communist party members. As Alexander Berkman put it:

"Kronstadt lived in the spirit of its holy crusade. It had abiding faith in the justice of its cause and felt itself the true defender of the Revolution. In this state of mind the sailors did not believe that the Government would attack them by force of arms.

"In the subconsciousness of these simple children of the soil and sea there perhaps germinated the feeling that not only through violence may victory be gained. The Slavic psychology seemed to believe that the justice of the cause and the strength of the revolutionary spirit must win. At any rate, Kronstadt refused to take the offensive. The Revolutionary Committee would not accept the insistent advice of the military experts to make an immediate landing on Oranienbaum, a fort of great strategic value. The Kronstadt sailors and soldiers aimed to establish free Soviets and were willing to defend their rights against attack; but they would not be aggressors."[21]

IV

THE KRONSTADT SAILORS, "THE PARTRIDGES"

Trotsky, the Soviet War Commissar, arrived in Petrograd on March 5th. His first act was an ultimatum in the name of the workers' and peasants' Government to Kronstadt, the fortress city, to submit voluntarily or be destroyed.[22] Trotsky's ultimatum was followed by a prikaz (order) in which he declared that he would "shoot like partridges"[23] all those who dared "raise their hand against the Socialist fatherland." By Socialist fatherland, of course, he meant the Communist party and its leaders. The divine right of kings had been questioned, which was punishable only by death. The righteous indignation of Bolshevik officialdom at the "rebels" and their "plot," the strenuous effort of the Communists to wrap themselves with the banner of the Revolution, cannot hide the fact that Trotsky was out to punish Kronstadt for only one crime: refusal to follow blindly orders from above—daring to question the wisdom of the leaders. Trotsky, and Zinoviev and Lenin, as the latter subsequently admitted,[24] knew full well that the Kronstadt sailors were not counter-revolutionists, that they never had associated with counter-revolutionists, and that they even refused assistance from Chernov, the leader of the Socialist-Revolutionaries. They knew this; nevertheless, they prepared to crush all those who doubted the infallibility of the Bolshevik leaders.

The ruler of Petrograd took precautionary measures to insure that the impending military campaign would be free of danger from the rear. The area was seething with discontent among the striking workers and the soldiers who sympathized with them. Therefore, the first step in preparation for military action against Kronstadt was the disarming of the Petrograd garrison. Those who had been rash enough to express solidarity with the besieged Kronstadt were removed summarily from the danger zone.

In "Living My Life," Emma Goldman describes the scene she saw from her window in the Hotel International. The arrested soldiers and workers were led away in small groups surrounded by strong detachments of Cheka troops.

"Their step had lost its spring, their hands hung at their sides, and their heads were bowed in grief.

"The Petrograd strikers were no longer feared by the authorities. They were weakened by slow starvation and their energy sapped. They were demoralized by the lies spread against them and their Kronstadt brothers, their spirit broken by the poison of doubt instilled by Bolshevik propaganda. They had no more fight nor faith left to come to the aid of their Kronstadt comrades who had so selflessly taken up their cause and who were about to give up their lives for them.

"Kronstadt was forsaken by Petrograd and cut off

from the rest of Russia. It stood alone. It could offer almost no resistance. 'It will go down at the first shot,' the Soviet Press proclaimed. They were mistaken. Kronstadt had actually not contemplated mutiny or resistance to the Soviet Government. To the very last moment it was determined to shed no blood. It appealed all the time for understanding and amicable settlement. But forced to defend itself against unprovoked military attack, it fought like a lion."[25]

Trotsky appointed General Tukhachevsky commander-in-chief of the Kronstadt attack. His assistants, drawn largely from the ranks of Tzarist forces whom Trotsky had pressed into the service of the Red Army some time ago, were seasoned military experts and strategists. There were also droves of Chekists "with three years' training in the art of murder,"[26] kursanti, specially picked battalions of Communists known for their blind obedience, and trusted troops brought in from various sections of the country. Unquestionably, Trotsky and his lieutenants believed that the "mutiny" would be easily quelled.

His ominous threat to shoot the Kronstadt sailors like partridges became the battle cry of the hosts gathering to storm the fortress-city for its reprehensible crime: the desire for democracy and decent human treatment.

V

THE ASSAULT UPON KRONSTADT

At the first signs of disaffection in Kronstadt, as already mentioned, the Petrograd Committee of Defense declared the latter city to be in an "extraordinary state of siege." No gatherings in the streets were allowed, no assemblies were permitted. Petrograders knew little of what was going on in Kronstadt. In frequent bulletins, the Communist press reported that the "Tsarist General Kozlovsky had organized a counter-revolutionary uprising in Kronstadt." Nevertheless rumors that the Government was preparing for military action against the fortress city were discounted. Only after the heavy guns of the Sestroretsk and Lissy Nos batteries had fired the first shots at Kronstadt at 6:45 in the evening of March 7th, did Petrograd realize that war had come.

Trotsky was well prepared for the assault. Into Petrograd he had brought his most trusted divisions—regiments of military academy students, the kursanti, Cheka detachments, and specially organized units of communists. There were 60,000 picked men altogether—a formidable army against one isolated fortress. They were stationed in the forts of Sestroretsk, Lissy Nos, Krasnaia Gorka and neighboring fortified positions. The best military experts, headed by General Tukhachevsky—the same Tukhachevsky who was destined to be executed by Stalin—were at Trotsky's disposal.

Forbidden to gather, the people of Petrograd were silenced; glumly and sulkily they waited for the worst.

On March 8th, the day after the first firing on Kronstadt, the *Izvestia* of the Kronstadt Soviet, in its issue No. 6, published the following appeal, under the heading "Let the Whole World Know:"

> "The first shot has been fired. . . . Standing up to his knees in the blood of the workers, Marshal Trotsky was the first to open fire against revolutionary Kronstadt which has risen against the autocracy of the Communists to establish the true power of the Soviets.
>
> "Without shedding a drop of blood, we, Red Army men, sailors, and workers of Kronstadt, have freed ourselves from the yoke of the Communists and even preserved their lives. By the threat of artillery they seek now to subject us again to their tyranny.
>
> "Not desiring bloodshed, we asked that non-partisan delegates of the Petrograd proletariat be sent to us, that they might learn that Kronstadt is fighting for the power of the Soviets. But the Communists have kept our demand from the workers of Petrograd, and now they have opened fire—the usual reply of the pseudo Workers' and Peasants' Government to the demands of the laboring masses.

"Let the workers of the whole world know that we, the defenders of Soviet Power, are safe-guarding the conquests of the Social Revolution. We will win or perish beneath the ruins of Kronstadt, fighting for the just cause of the laboring masses.

"The workers of the world will be our judges. The blood of the innocent will fall upon the heads of the Communist fanatics drunk with authority.

"Long live the Power of the Soviets!"[27]

Additional insight into the psychological make-up of the embattled sailors is afforded by their commemoration of Women Workers' Day (established as an international holiday August 27, 1910, at a women's socialist conference in Copenhagen). On March 8th, while Petrograd's batteries hammered continuously at the fortress-city, the following greeting was transmitted by radio to the working women of the world:

"Today is a universal holiday—Women Workers' Day. We of Kronstadt send, amid the thunder of cannon, our fraternal greetings to the workingwomen of the world. . . . May you soon accomplish your liberation from every form of violence and oppression. . . . Long live the free revolutionary workingwomen! Long live the Socialist Revolution throughout the world!"[28]

The Communist rulers had drawn an iron curtain around Kronstadt in an attempt to prevent the world from hearing the voice of the Russian people, for whom the sailors spoke so eloquently. The lies broadcast from Moscow, accusing them of counter-revolution and White conspiracy, could not permanently extinguish the purity of motives which prompted the Kronstadt sailors to revolt. They wanted a free Russia, they had unbounded faith in the Soviets—freely elected, democratically ruled Soviets, councils representing the laboring masses—not domination by one party. The pages of *Izvestia*, the short-lived official organ of the Kronstadt Provisional Revolutionary Committee, testify to the true spirit of those under siege and the intriguing, conniving, bestial machinations of the Communist rulers.* What we now say and think of those Communist rulers was written thirty years ago by the Kronstadt martyrs.

Here we quote another editorial in the March 8 (No. 6) issue of *Izvestia* under the heading "We and They:"

> "Not knowing how to retain the power that is falling from their hands, the Communists resort to the vilest provocative means. Their contemptible press has mobilized all its forces to incite the masses and put the Kronstadt movement in the light of a White guard conspiracy. Now a clique of shameless villains has sent word to the world that 'Kronstadt has sold itself to Finland.' Their newspapers spit fire and poison, and because they have failed to persuade the proletariat that Kronstadt is in the hands of counter-revolutionists, they are now trying to play on the nationalistic feeling.

> "The whole world already knows from our radios what the Kronstadt garrison and workers are fighting for. But the Communists are striving to pervert the meaning of events and thus mislead our Petrograd brothers.

> "Petrograd is surrounded by the bayonets of the

* For an illuminating story on the abuse of the white flag by the Communists during the war with the Kronstadters, see Appendix VI.

kursanti and Party 'guards,' and Maliuta Skuratov*-
Trotsky does not permit the delegates of the nonparti-
san workers and soldiers to go to Kronstadt. He fears
they would learn the whole truth there, and that truth
would immediately sweep the Communists away and
the thus-enlightened laboring masses would take the
power into their hands.

"That is the reason that the Petro-Soviet (Soviet
of Petrograd) did not reply to our radio-telegram in
which we asked that really impartial comrades be sent
to Kronstadt.

"Fearing for their own skins, the leaders of the
Communists suppress the truth and disseminate the lie
that White guardists are active in Kronstadt, that the
Kronstadt proletariat has sold itself to Finland and to

----

* MALIUTA SKURATOV, a favorite nobleman of Ivan the Terrible,
head of the Oprichnina. Its members, called Oprichniki, were hired retain-
ers who roved the country, killing and plundering the property of any
noble whom the Tsar suspected of disloyalty. The avowed purpose of the
Oprichnina was to forestall the development of an independent baronial
class. Thus, the Tsar reduced his subjects, from the old noble families to
the lowest serfs, to the common denominator of slaves, dependent upon
his slightest whims.

The Oprichnina had its own special court, its ministerial offices, its
own army, its own special police—at first one thousand and later six thousand in number.

(The Bolshevik creation, the Cheka, subsequently called the NKVD,
was formed on the same principles and adopted the Oprichnina methods
of dealing with the native bourgeoisie.)

The Oprichnik police, clothed in black, rode black horses and carried
a dog's head at their saddle-bow and a broom, which symbolized their mis-
sion to clear the land of robbery and disloyalty.

The Oprichniki of Bolshevik time, the Cheka, also wore black leather
coats or jackets, appeared at their victim's doors in black automobiles, nick-
named "the black crows," in the middle of the night, and they were armed
with Naguans.

Maliuta Skuratov, whose very name struck terror in the hearts of the
people, was called the "eye" and "ear" and the punitive, avenging "hand"
of the Tsar that smote his enemies, actual and potential. Dzerzinski, the
Maliuta Skuratov of his day, was the head of the Bolshevik State Security,
often referred to as "the fiery sword of the Revolution."

French spies, and that the Finns have already organized an army in order to attack Petrograd with the aid of the Kronstadt myatezhniki (mutineers), and so forth.

"To all this we can reply only this: All power to the Soviets! Keep your hands off them, the hands red with the blood of the martyrs of liberty who have died fighting against the White guardists, the landlords, and the bourgeoisie!"[29]

THE FALL OF KRONSTADT

As was pointed out earlier, the Kronstadt sailors coun-
tenanced no aggressive moves in their plans for protecting
the city against government attack. Although their military
position called for certain aggressive actions, even in this
purely defensive campaign, the sailors held back for political
reasons: so that their actions would not be interpreted as a
war waged against the Government, but rather as a defense
against the government's attack. There was an element of
martyrdom in the decision. The logic of good strategy required—nay, dictated—the immediate capture of the fortified
port of Oranienbaum (about 37 miles from Petrograd on
the southern shores of the Gulf of Finland) to prevent complete isolation from the mainland. But Kronstadters refused
to take this step.

"The failure of Kronstadt to take Oranienbaum
gave the Government an opportunity to strengthen

the fortress with its trusted regiments, eliminate the 'infected' parts of the garrison, and execute the leaders of the aerial squadron which was about to join the Kronstadt rebels. Later, the Bolsheviki used the fortress as a vantage point of attack against Kronstadt.

"Among those executed in Oranienbaum were: Kolossov, division chief of the Red Navy airmen and chairman of the Provisional Revolutionary Committee just organized in Oranienbaum; Balabanov, secretary of the Committee; and Committee members Romanov, Vladimirov, etc."[30]

Kronstadt was designed to serve Petrograd as an outpost of defense against enemies approaching from the sea. Its guns aimed westward. However, the rear of Kronstadt, facing Petrograd, was unprotected and now proved to be the city's weakest point. Furthermore, the builders of the fortress had figured that if it ever fell into enemy hands, it could be bombarded successfully from the coastal forts of Krasnaia Gorka (see map), whose guns were trained upon Kronstadt. (The Government held Krasnaia Gorka).

The moral force was on the side of the sailors. But moral force alone could not overcome the batteries pointing at Kronstadt from three directions. The weather was severe at this time of year. Thick ice covered the Finland Gulf, making possible an approach to the city by infantry.

On the evening of March 7th, artillery bombardment against Kronstadt was followed by an attempt to storm the fortress. Picked Communist troops, clad in white capes to camouflage them in their stealthy march across the snow, attacked from north and south. A terrible snowstorm broke out. The Finnish Gulf was pitch dark. The Communists drove to the walls of Kronstadt, but death sought them out in the night as artillery and machine-gun fire spurted from the fortress. The attack was repulsed, but not before the snow had become crimson with the blood of the many who died in that first battle.

The Kronstadters mourned the spilling of innocent blood, the blood of soldiers, cadets and workers who were duped into believing that they were fighting counter-revolutionists, White guards, and enemies of the Revolution. As they expressed it in an editorial in the Kronstadt *Izvestia* of March 8:

> "We did not want to shed the blood of our brothers, and we did not fire a single shot until compelled to do so. We had to defend the just cause of the laboring people and to shoot—to shoot at our own brothers sent to certain death by Communists who have grown fat at the expense of the people.
>
> ". . . To your misfortune there broke a terrific snowstorm and black night shrouded everything in darkness. Nevertheless, the Communist executioners, counting no cost, drove you along the ice, threatening you in the rear with their machine guns operated by Communist detachments.
>
> "Many of you perished that night on the icy vastness of the Gulf of Finland. And when day broke and the storm quieted down, only pitiful remnants of you, worn and hungry, hardly able to move, came to us clad in your white shrouds.
>
> "Early in the morning there were already about a thousand of you and later in the day a countless number. Dearly you have paid with your blood for this adventure, and after your failure Trotsky rushed back to Petrograd to drive new martyrs to slaughter—for cheaply he gets workers' and peasants' blood!"[31]

How well was Kronstadt prepared for battle with the Government forces? The garrison, consisting of less than 14,000 men, 10,000 of whom were sailors, had to defend a widespread front, many forts and batteries scattered over the vast area of the Gulf. The provisions in the besieged city were scanty. If they had controlled Oranienbaum, they would have been well provided with food, for 50,000 poods of wheat belonging to Kronstadt were storaged there. (A Russian pood is equivalent to about 36 English pounds). Unfortunately, Oranienbaum was in Bolshevik hands.

Day and night, the Communists attacked. Fresh Government troops were thrown into battle continuously, while the garrison fought on without relief or replacements. There were no airlifts or paratroopers in those days. Within the fortress, the ranks of the defenders grew thinner as exhaustion, scanty rations, long sleepless nights on guard in the winter cold sapped the vitality of Kronstadt. Yet they kept on fiercely, stubbornly, defending their beloved city. Desperately they hoped that other Russian cities, at the very least Petrograd, the nearest to them, would be fired by their heroic example and would rise too, to liberate themselves and come to Kronstadt's aid.

The March 11th, 1921, issue of *Kronstadt Izvestia* carried this heartrending "Appeal to Comrades, Workers and Peasants:"

"Comrades, Workers, Kronstadt is fighting for you, for the hungry, the cold, the naked. . . . Kronstadt has raised the banner of rebellion and it is confident that tens of millions of workers and peasants will respond to its call. It cannot be that the daybreak which has begun in Kronstadt should not become bright sunshine for the whole of Russia. It cannot be that the Kronstadt explosion should fail to arouse the whole of Russia and first of all, Petrograd."[32]

But Russia remained silent and the will of Petrograd was paralyzed by hunger, fear, and the utter despair of its impotence.

Every night, under cover of darkness, the Communists continued their attacks. Artillery unceasingly bombarded Kronstadt from the southern and northern coasts. On the night of March 12-13, again employing white capes to camouflage their movements, the Communists sent in from the South cadets of the Red Officer Schools—without success. Kronstadt was fighting magnificently, despite lack of food and men and rest.

Most fearsome to Kronstadt were the simultaneous attacks from north, south and east. As explained previously, her stationary batteries could defend the city only from the west and she lacked even an ice-cutter to forestall the approach across the frozen Gulf.

March 16th brought the last general attack upon Kronstadt. The battle plan had been worked out in minutest detail under the direction of Commander-in-Chief Tukhachevsky and the field staff of the Southern Corps. As night descended, the Bolsheviks launched a concentrated assault upon the forts from three sides simultaneously—north, south and east. The young kursanti, who had been instilled with a fanatic hatred toward the "counter-revolutionists," attacked in column after column with utter disregard for their own and their enemies' life.

On the morning of March 17th, the battle was over. A number of forts had been captured. The Bolsheviki had broken through Kronstadt's weakest spot, the Petrograd Gates, the unfortified eastern section facing Petrograd. Here, the Government forces poured into the city—and then began a brutal slaughter of the conquered sailors, the most despicable, vengeful phase of the campaign.

Even after the breakthrough the defenders of Kronstadt did not surrender. They continued to fight against overwhelming odds. Now, however, the numerous Communists in the city, whom the sailors had spared, betrayed their generosity and joined the Government forces. Commissar of the Baltic Fleet Kuzmin and Chairman of the Kronstadt Soviet Vassiliev, released from prison by the Communists, also joined the Government troops and participated in the hand-to-hand street fighting with the Kronstadt defenders. The desperate struggle continued late into the night. The streets and forts of Kronstadt were strewn with the killed and wounded. It was estimated that 18,000 of the rebels had been killed. Also thousands of the government troops paid with their lives. The city lay prostrate before the enemy.

Tukhachevsky later declared that in all the years of war and civil war he had not witnessed such carnage.

"It was not a battle," he said, "it was an inferno. . . . The sailors fought like wild beasts. I cannot understand where they found the might for such rage. Each house where they were located had to be taken by storm."[33]

Dibenko, a sailor, was appointed Commissar of Kronstadt. He was given absolute powers to mop up the rebel city, a cleansing job which the Cheka took over happily. An orgy of vengeance ensued: people were shot in batches; others were sent to jails in Petrograd to be disposed of later by firing squads. Many were condemned to prisons and concentration camps in the frozen outlands of Archangel or the dungeons of the over-hot region of Turkestan.

"Thousands fell before firing squads during the period, for the continuing existence of the Bolshevik regime was threatened. According to the 'Frankfurter Zeitung,' from February 28 to March 6, 1921, 2,500 soldiers of the Petrograd garrison were shot. According to the sailors who escaped to Finland, executions were carried out on the ice under the walls of the Kronstadt fortress. In Oranienbaum, a summer-resort 37 miles from Petrograd, on the Southern shores of the Finnish Bay, 1,400 were executed. (Reported in 'Poslednie Novosti,' No. 281). Available information proves that 6 priests were shot for participation in the Kronstadt Rebellion."[34]

The following passage appeared in "The Truth about Kronstadt," a book published in Prague in 1921.

"To present some semblance of legality to its butchery of Kronstadt, the Communists in Petrograd have arranged a 'trial' of 13 Kronstadt rebels picked at random from the many arrested. The court having 'duly' taken into consideration all 'circumstances' and 'crimes' of the accused, sentenced them to death. The sentence, having been proclaimed final, without right of appeal, in view of the fact that revolutionary order is being established in Kronstadt, had to be carried out immediately.

"The following Kronstadt rebels have been sentenced to death and shot:

DENYER, 24 years old, assistant commander of the warship *Sevastopol*, former midshipman, former nobleman of the Petrograd Government region.
Artillerymen, of the same warship *Sevastopol:*
MAZUROV, 28 years old, former lieutenant, former nobleman of the Petrograd Government region.

BECKMAN, 23 years old, ship pilot, former mid
man, former nobleman from the Government ᴏᵢ
Perm.

LEVITZKY, turret commander, 35 years old, staff
captain, former nobleman.

SOFRONOV, 27 years old, former midshipman, former nobleman from the Government of Tver.

TIMONOV, 37 years old, former clergyman, from
the Sevsky district of the Government of Orlov.

Sailors, members of the ship's committee:

SUGANKOV, 25 years old, peasant, from the village
Staraya Kemenka, volost-Stavinsky, Chernigove-
uyezd, Government of Gomel.

STEPANOV, 33 years old, peasant, village Pestovo,
volost-Vysotzty-uyezd, Government of Novgorod.

YEFREMOV, 29 years old, peasant, village Orla,
volost-Narovsk uyzed-Yamburg, Government of
Petrograd.

VOROBYOV, 29 years old, peasant, village Moskov-
sky, uyezd-Krapivinsk, Government of Tula.

SPESHIN, 30 years old, peasant, volost Dragunsk,
uyezd-Karabchevsk, Government of Briansk.

CHERNOUSOV, 23 years old, peasant, village Za-
bologye, volost-Ustdensk, uyezd-Igumensk, Government of Minsk "[35]

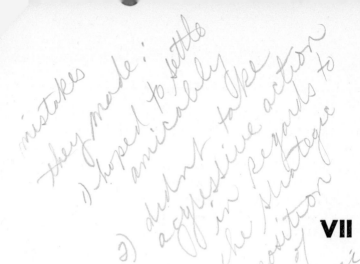

mistakes made:
they made to settle
1) hoped to settle
amicably
2) didn't take action to
aggressive acts to
in strategic
the position
position of
oranien
bau
planning
springtime

VII

THE LESSON OF KRONSTADT

3) No real

3) No real planning

There are certain lessons to be drawn from the failure of the Kronstadt sailors to win their battle for freedom.

Even with their knowledge of what made a Communist ruler tick, the Kronstadt leaders hoped to settle the conflict amicably; they were willing to believe that the Communists possessed some sense of justice and respect for freedom other than their own. They failed to learn in time the nature of Bolshevism. Freedom means sharing power, allowing it to be open to competition and subject to limitations, even at the risk of its possible loss. Too late for its own good, Kronstadt realized that the Bolsheviks could never permit this.

Other failures resulted from Kronstadt's fatal psychological miscalculation of the nature of the enemy—the failure to take advantage of strategic positions, the failure to act aggressively when only aggressiveness and speed could generate enthusiasm and bring about the onrush of followers and supporters.

As one ardent revolutionary expressed it:

4) y knew nature of the beast.

". . . Every uprising has against it the powerful machinery of the State. The Government is able to concentrate in its hands the sources of supply and the means of communication. No time must be given the Government to make use of its powers. Rebellion should be vigorous, striking unexpectedly and determinedly. It must not remain localized, for that means stagnation. It must broaden and develop. A rebellion that localizes itself, plays the waiting policy, or puts itself on the defensive, is inevitably doomed to defeat."[35a]

"The Truth about Kronstadt," discussing the military aspect of the defense of Kronstadt, had the following to say:

"Had the Kronstadt sailors and their leaders planned the uprising, they would not have met with disaster; had they really foreseen the necessity of taking up arms, they would not have started it in the month of March. They knew that the fortress could be reached by a large army marching across the solid ice surrounding them. Had they waited a couple of months, the spring sun would have melted the ice. The Kronstadt fortress would have been unapproachable from land. With a powerful fleet at their disposal they could have threatened the city of Petrograd. (Had they not sealed the fate of the Kerensky Government by having the battleship *Aurora* threaten to bombard the Winter Palace?)

"They did not even take steps to break the ice around the fortress as a matter of precaution. They did nothing, because it was inconceivable to them that the Government would attack them and because they relied upon public opinion, upon the resentment of a large part of the people.

"Had they planned the attack they would have been militarily justified to attack first. They would have caught the Bolsheviks unprepared and confused. Had not the first battalions sent against the fortress gone over to the Kronstadters or refused to fight? However, the Communists in Moscow and Petrograd realized the danger of such an attack and decided to act swiftly to suppress the revolt."

Another valuable lesson learned from the crushing of the Kronstadt rebellion is the fact that the Bolshevik Government would not hesitate to drown in blood any attempt to create a movement for freely elected Soviets, thus revealing the true character of Communist dictatorship.

However, while refusing to grant the demands of its own people, the Bolshevik Government was willing to make almost any compromise with the capitalist world: it signed the Riga peace treaty, whereby a population of 12 million Ukrainians and White Russians was turned over to the mercies of Poland. It was ready to give up such basic Communist policies as forced requisitions; it was ready to introduce free trade, and offer great concessions to capitalists in order to guarantee its own survival. But, to its own people, the Bolsheviks refused to grant freely elected Soviets, or freedom of speech and press to the other revolutionary parties.

The NEP, or New Economic Policy, which we shall examine later, was formulated at the Tenth All-Russian Congress of the Communist Party, in session in Moscow at the time of the Kronstadt uprising. Not that the Bolshevik rulers were convinced that their methods had brought Russia's millions to the brink of ruin, hunger and despair; they blamed others for their failures.

Lenin admitted to the Communists gathered at the 10th

All-Russian Congress of the Party, with the bland cynicism of the dictator, that every thoughtful person knew all along that "the Kronstadt men did not really want the counter-revolutionists. BUT NEITHER DID THEY WANT US."[36] And for this they perished.

"The Lenin policy of the NEP," the large Soviet Encyclopoedia remarks with satisfaction, "deprived the counter-revolutionists of any grounds for agitation in the villages and under the leadership of the proletariat strengthened the unity of the working class and the peasantry."[37]

VIII

THE NEW ECONOMIC POLICY (NEP)

The New Economic Policy, or NEP for short, was the direct result of the Kronstadt Rebellion in the sense that the upheaval in Kronstadt brought home to the Bolsheviks most clearly and forcefully that their economic policy was a complete failure and that something had to be done to remedy the situation if the Government was to survive.

The Kronstadt Rebellion was the culmination of the frenzy to which the people were roused as a result of the Government's economic tyranny. The economic demands of the Kronstadt sailors, contained in their 15 point resolution of March 1, 1921, underscored the country's minimum needs; in addition to freely elected Soviets and the abolition of privileges for the Communists, they demanded freer trade and mitigation of Government regulations on how villages were to carry on their farming and dispose of their products. The official food policy had brought almost complete destruction to the peasant economy. Indeed, the food dictatorship established by the Government's decree of March 13, 1918, reminded one, by its thorough-going methods, of the Tartar Khans who overran the country six hundred years earlier. All surplus agricultural products above the amount needed for individual consumption and for sowing were to be handed over immediately to the State. In practice, however, many peasants were fleeced not only of their minimum food requirements but also of seeds for the next year's harvest. The men in the Department of Food Army were not particular in their methods. That armed force was composed mainly of town-workers and soldiers, in detachments of 75 men. Each detachment carried three machine guns and as the men marched through the villages, they were guilty of all sorts of brutalities. True, the Government attempted to assess contributions according to statistical data on the peasants' normal production capacity. But such data was incomplete. The Government required food for the cities; the Food Detachments had orders to get it, and they wasted little time or sympathetic understanding on estimations of the peasants' surpluses.

In some districts, the peasants responded to this policy of force with force. Many food commissars were slain. But the peasant resorted to a far more effective method of reprisal: he reduced his sowing acreage. Why plant more than his need, when every extra pood of grain would be confiscated by Government henchmen? He drastically limited his cultivation, growing only the amount he required for himself and his family. In December, 1920, Lenin declared: "Our chief task now is to know how to raise agricultural productivity" by State compulsion. The 8th Congress of the All-Russian Soviets decided that henceforth the State would define the area of yearly planting and the peasant would be compelled to sow according to plan. This measure, however, was not put into effect at that time. The old Communist experiments, whose results had proven so tragic and costly for the national economy, had to be suspended temporarily.

If the Government had supplied the peasants with the manufactured products they required, there would have been no need for food requisition. But owing to the industrial collapse (brought on in part by Bolshevik policies), demands could not be met. During 1920, the Government could supply only 5 per cent of the peasant requirements in the Ukraine for manufactured goods, agricultural machinery, nails, axes, etc. And with the prohibition against private trading, needs could not be satisfied in the open market. Furthermore, the nationalization of industry and trade had created an enormous bureaucracy. "In 1919 the State was obliged to support no less than 23,000,000 people. In 1920, this figure rose to 35,000,000."[38] The Government, in the face of all these difficulties, determined to obtain food from the peasant by force.

Peasant uprisings against Communist oppression broke out in all sections of the Soviet Union, especially in Siberia, the Volga districts, and the Black Land regions. The Moscow area did not escape disorders. The Petrograd workers, more independent in spirit than those in any other city of Russia because of their revolutionary traditions, displayed such strong resentment that the Government became deeply disturbed. When the Kronstadt garrison, the "beauty and pride of the Russian Revolution," finally demonstrated that they were prepared to resist further lawlessness by the Government, the Government took stock of the situation—but first it ruthlessly crushed the Kronstadt rebellion.

March 15th, while Kronstadt was still under bombardment, Lenin declared to the Communists assembled in the Tenth Assembly of the Communist Party:

"We know that only by agreement with the peasantry can we save the socialistic revolution in Russia as long as it has not yet advanced into other countries. The peasantry is dissatisfied with the present form of our relations with it. It does not want these forms of relations and will not let them continue in this way. This is indisputable. The peasant's will has been definitely expressed. We must reckon with this. We are sufficiently sober politicians to be able to speak our mind. Let us reconsider our policy vis-a-vis the peasantry. Essentially the position is this. We must either satisfy the 'middle' peasant economically and allow freedom of exchange, or else maintain the power of the proletariat (i.e., the Communist Party. E.P.) in Russia, which is impossible by reason of the delay of the International Revolution. Economically, we can't do this."[38a]

The result was the New Economic Policy (NEP) which introduced a few changes in the country's economic policy. Lenin recognized that the Kronstadt crisis, although prompted in part by economic considerations, was definitely political in character and menaced the existence of Communist power. Therefore, while yielding slight concessions in the economic field, the Communists were fully determined to maintain political dictatorship. For the moment, the NEP seemed a great achievement, but in reality it turned out to be of very limited benefit. It was as though Lenin, the coachman, while holding the reins of the Russian troika, decided to slacken the horse's pace from a full gallop to an easy trot. The horses felt relieved of the steady hard pulling of the reins and enjoyed the comparative freedom, but the reins remained in the over-bearing coachman's hands.

Bukharin, one of the bright stars in the Communist firmament in the nineteen-twenties, discussing the NEP, said:

> "We must strengthen our power and make no political concession, but, on the contrary, we must make as many economic concessions as possible. Opportunists have formed the opinion that at first we make economic concessions and then political. As a matter of fact we make economic concessions in order not to be forced to political concessions. We cannot allow equality of rights between the peasants and the workers (i.e., of towns)."[39]

Another prominent member of the party, Aleksei Rykov, expressed it even more clearly:

> "The poletarian state cannot consistently allow freedom of trade and the development of capitalism. At most, it can only allow these things to a very limited extent, and even then, only on condition of state regulation of private trade and private capitalistic initiative."[40]

For the people, the New Economic Policy meant a breathing spell from the intense rigors of the dictatorship. The peasant was freed from unlimited requisitions of his surplus produce; instead, he paid a fixed tax, at first in grain, meat, and other products, later in money. Private trade was legalized, though the Government retained its monopoly of foreign trade. One of the earliest measures of the NEP was the partial denationalization of small industries, such as handcrafts, etc. However, the State owned all other industry and strove to stimulate it with Russian and foreign capital. The Government granted leases and concessions to foreign businessmen to develop mineral, industrial and commercial enterprises, without letting out of its direct control railways, plants of heavy industry, etc., what it called "the commanding heights." To increase productivity, these industries were reorganized in the form of trusts. They remained State institutions, as before, but were to be operated along business lines, i.e., they were to enjoy certain privileges customary in private business in capitalistic countries. However, the foreign concession policy failed to bring anticipated results. Too many strings were attached to dissipate the general distrust and scepticism of the Soviet State felt by most foreign businessmen and investors. By the early thirties, all foreign concessions came to an end, except the coal and oil concessions to the Japanese in the Russian half of Sakhalin Island. These concessions were actually a political accommodation, since they were the price paid for Japan's abandonment of military occupation of Northern Sakhalin in 1925.

The New Economic Policy brought a temporary and partial improvement to the national economy.

By 1928, however, it started to fall into disrepute and was given up entirely in 1929. Not because it worsened the country's economic position; not because it was detrimental to the welfare of the peasants and workers as a whole; but, again, for purely political reasons, for the same reasons that the Kronstadt sailors were sacrificed. The NEP produced a certain measure of prosperity in the villages. And when the peasant found his condition improved, he soon realized his significance in the national economy. He began to put out demands, which became more and more urgent, and he insisted upon a share in Government. The Government, dependent upon the peasant's food and taxes, could no longer ignore him and still less apply the old police methods of the pre-NEP days.

In the cities, a new bourgeois class had arisen—the nep-men, contractors, traders, and new managerial groups. They, too, aware of how greatly the Government depended upon them, started to feel and show their strength. The Bolsheviks were confronted again with the problem of sharing their power with new social groups. The Government's answer could be foreseen and foretold. The strong ruling caste would not permit its power to slip from its hands. To recall the words of Bukharin:

"... Opportunists have formed the opinion that at first we make economic concessions and then political. *AS A MATTER OF FACT WE MAKE ECONOMIC CONCESSIONS IN ORDER NOT TO BE FORCED TO POLITICAL CONCESSIONS. WE CANNOT ALLOW EQUALITY OF RIGHTS BETWEEN THE PEASANTS AND THE WORKERS (i.e., THE COMMUNIST PARTY. E.P.). ..."* [41]

"Socialism" must prevail. It is hard to set a date for the end of the NEP; it began to fall apart in 1928 and in 1929 it was completely wiped out, and the classes which represented it were exterminated economically and to some extent physically with a ruthlessness befitting the party of the "proletariat."

IX

WHAT DO THE BOLSHEVIKS SAY ABOUT
THE KRONSTADT REBELLION?

The tendency of Soviet historical literature has been to minimize the Kronstadt Rebellion as much as possible, to ignore it completely, or to present it in such a biased, distorted version as to leave the student seeking the true facts in despair.

Before us is the official 3-volume history of the USSR, written by Prof. A. M. Pankratova,* the text-book of the

---

* ANNA M. PANKRATOVA, Soviet historian who assisted in the "rewriting of Stalinist history books, died yesterday (May 25th, 1957) after a long illness . . . her age was 60. . . . In the autumn of 1956, Mrs. Pankratova directed the preparation of a new "Guide for Teachers" under which the country's pre-Communist history was rewritten. History lessons in schools were to be RADICALLY CHANGED TO REMOVE THE GLOSS PUT BY STALIN ON RUSSIA'S PRE-REVOLUTIONARY HISTORY AND PARTICULARLY ON SOME CZARS." (Our emphasis. E.P.)

(From a dispatch from London to the New York Times May 27, 1957.)

Soviet high schools, on which the Russian youth is brought up today. And what are the high school students taught about the crucial events of March, 1921, when the "pride and glory of the Revolution" was in arms against the regime? The entire Kronstadt affair occupies one small page in the above-mentioned official history. Following is a verbatim translation of the complete entry:

"KRONSTADT MUTINY

"Domestic and foreign enemies of the Soviet rule hurried to take advantage of the economic and political difficulties. The counter-revolutionary elements—the Mensheviks, the Es-Ar's, the Whiteguard, the bourgeois nationalists—revived their activities. They camouflaged themselves as non-party men and brought forth, not the previous slogan—Down with the Soviets —but a new one: For the Soviets, but without the Communists!

"Particularly clear became these new tactics of the class-enemy in March, 1921, during the counter-revolutionary rebellion in Kronstadt.

"Kronstadt was the main base of the Baltic Fleet. During the revolution and civil war the Baltic Fleet had sent to the front many thousands of fighters supremely devoted to the revolution. Reinforcements of the Fleet during that time consisted of chance, often declassed, elements not quite hardened by the revolution. Political education in the Baltic fleet was badly organized. Trotskyites had made their way to the

---

We doubt very much whether in the new history books Mrs. Pankratova removed that which was much more than just a "gloss," from her false interpretation of the Kronstadt rebellion. The history of this rebellion will not be de-stalinized by the Communists. The layers of falsehoods in which it is tightly wrapped will remain untouched. From the point of view of the Bolsheviks the rebellion is still a counter-revolutionary act.

leadership of the Fleet, bringing decadence with them into the small party-stratum of communists among the sailors. Camouflaged as non-party men, the S-R's, the Mensheviks, the Anarchists intensified in the Fleet their subversive activities. They succeeded in carrying a counter-revolutionary resolution at the meeting of March 1st. Kronstadt was in the hands of a gang of Whiteguard-agents.

"Whiteguard military experts headed by General Koslovsky had directed the military operations of the Kronstadt rebels. The entire counter-revolution, internal and external, supported the rebels of Kronstadt. In Paris the White emigres collected money and provisions for them. The American Red Cross transported supplies of provisions under its flag to Kronstadt. The cadet (Constitutional Democrat) Miliukov supplied the Kronstadt counter-revolutionaries with a slogan: 'Soviets without the Communists.'

" 'Soviets without the Communists,' said Comrade Stalin, exposing the manoeuvres of the class-enemies, 'such was then the watch-word of Miliukov, the head of the Russian counter-revolution. The counter-revolutionaries understood that the crux of the matter was not the Soviets themselves, but, above all, who were to lead them! (Stalin, Articles and Speeches. Partisdat. 1934. p. 217).

"For seventeen days Kronstadt was in the hands of the White Guards. The Defense Committee of the Petrograd Fortified Region failed to suppress the rebellion in its inception. Seven days Zinoviev carried on negotiations with the traitors to their country, thus giving them time to fortify themselves.

"Best units of the Red Army were sent to smash the Kronstadt counter-revolution, and to support them 300 delegates of the 10th Congress of the Party headed by K. E. Voroshilov were sent. March 16th, under incessant fire of machine and artillery guns, lines of revolutionary fighters, clad in white capes as camouflage, made their way to the main Kronstadt fortifications on the brittle ice of the bay blasted by enemy fire. Voroshilov was in the first lines of the storming columns, giving an example of Bolshevik courage and heroism.

"March 17th the nest of the Kronstadt counter-revolution was liquidated."

This is the way history is written in a Bolshevik state!

Another text book with which every Russian student must be thoroughly familiar is the "History of the Communist Party of the Soviet Union," referred to among the irreverent as "the bible." While we cannot expect objectivity from Prof. Pankratova in her authorized history of the USSR, it is interesting to note her "deviations" from the official text of the "History of the Communist Party." In its discussion of the Kronstadt rebellion, the latter volume contains no mention of Trotsky or Zinoviev. Prof. Pankratova, however, in her zeal to please her masters, manufactured some tall tales and overplayed her hand.

"Trotskyites," she wrote, "had made their way to the leadership of the fleet, bringing decadence with them into the small party-stratum of communists among the sailors."

By 1948, when Pankratova's History was republished, Trotsky's name had become an epithet to describe anyone accused of disaffection with the regime. But the world did not forget that it was Trotsky who suppressed the Kronstadt Rebellion with an iron hand, promising to shoot the sailors like partridges.

"Seven days Zinoviev carried on negotiations with the

traitors to their country," wrote Prof. Pankratova, "thus giving them time to fortify themselves."

Was it because she realized how weak her case was before the judgment of the world that Prof. Pankratova evoked the shadows of the disgraced and liquidated President of the Petrograd Soviet and the first head of the Third International? In any event, her fabrications have no bases in fact. All the evidence shows that the Kronstadt sailors sent a Committee of 30 to Petrograd to explain Kronstadt's demands to the workers and garrison there and to request that non-partisan delegates be sent by the Petrograd proletariat to the fortress city to learn the actual state of affairs. This Committee was arrested by the Bolsheviks in Petrograd, as mentioned earlier, and its fate remains a mystery.

Alexander Berkman, in his pamphlet "The Kronstadt Rebellion" (pp. 32-33), tells us that a group of Anarchists in Petrograd made a final attempt to induce the Bolsheviki to reconsider their decision to attack Kronstadt. They felt it their duty to the Revolution, he reports, to make an effort, even if it proved hopeless, to prevent the imminent massacre. On March 5th, they sent a protest to the Committee of Defense (whose Chairman was Zinoviev), pointing out the peaceful intentions and just demands of Kronstadt, reminding the Communists of the sailors' heroic revolutionary history, and suggesting a method of settling the dispute in a manner befitting comrades and revolutionists. This document reads in part:

> ". . . Concerning the conflict between the Soviet Government and the workers and sailors, we hold that it must be settled not by force of arms but by means of comradely, fraternal revolutionary agreement. Resorting to bloodshed, on the part of the Soviet Government, will not—in the given situation—intimidate

or quiet the workers. On the contrary, it will serve only to aggravate matters and will strengthen the hands of the Entente and of internal counter-revolution. . . .

". . . We hereby submit to you the following proposition: let a Commission be selected to consist of five persons, inclusive of two Anarchists. The Commission is to go to Kronstadt to settle the dispute by peaceful means. In the given situation this is the most radical method. It will be of international revolutionary significance.

	Alexander Berkman
Petrograd	Emma Goldman
March 5, 1921	Perkus
	Petrovsky "

Zinoviev, informed that a document pertaining to the Kronstadt problem had been submitted to the Soviet of Defense, sent his personal representative for it. Whether the letter was discussed with the Committee of Defense was never learned by the writers of the letter. At any rate, no action was taken in the matter. And this should dispose of the official lie that Zinoviev carried on negotiations with the Kronstadters for seven days.

The "fact" of Zinoviev's negotiations affording the Kronstadt sailors time to fortify themselves is just another sample of communist cynicism and perversion of history, and demonstrates the dictator's predilection for accusing others of actions he contemplates taking himself or has already taken. Hoping until the last moment that the Government would not resort to arms and avoiding every act that might lead to their being considered rebels, the Kronstadters did nothing that would insure adequate protection—they even

refused to take Oranienbaum, which would have strengthened them immeasurably. On the other hand, Trotsky, Zinoviev and Tukhachevsky quietly removed all garrisons of
doubtful allegiance from Petrograd and replaced them with
loyal contingents for the day of reckoning with the "mutineers," as the "historian" herself admits.

". . . Whiteguard military experts headed by General Kozlovsky," says Pankratova, "directed the military operations of Kronstadt . . ."

Here she repeats the official lie first uttered in March,
1921. Of course, the "historian" Pankratova knew that the
Kozlovsky story was a pure invention, that the old feeble
general, a Trotsky appointee, did not and could not have
any influence with the Kronstadt sailors. The Bolsheviks
needed a scapegoat and a scarecrow in the form of an old
Tsarist general. So they produced one.

As for the Kronstadt sailors being counter-revolutionists,
how could Prof. Pankratova overlook Lenin's statement
(made at the Tenth Congress of the Communist Party three
days after the Rebellion was put down) that "the Kronstadt
men did not really want the counter-revolutionists. But
neither did they want us"?

Of course, we must assume that she was familiar with
Lenin's statement, but to have quoted it would have meant
upsetting the whole structure of official lies in reference to
the Kronstadt Rebellion.

The role that Klim Voroshilov played in the crushing of
Kronstadt is a complete mystery. As far as we could ascertain, no mention of him was made at the time in the Communist press. The centre of the stage was occupied by
Trotsky, who organized the military forces, and behind him

stood Tukhachevsky, who planned the strategy and conducted the campaign. But no word of Klim Voroshilov. The
only explanation is that he was glorified in the official his-
tories at a later date to supplant Trotsky as the leading
figure. If Voroshilov actually was in the "first lines of the
storming columns," nobody at the time singled him out for it.
He finally achieved his credit by subterfuge. He was infil-
trated into the official history book through the back door as
an after-thought.

* * *

It is pertinent to mention that the Kronstadt "affair"
plagued Trotsky during his exile in Mexico. Here, the former "partridge-shooter" had to account for his role before
the court of public opinion when he asked to be defended
against Stalin's attacks. He was outraged that the "episode"
was revived and that people dared to question him about his
past.

". . . It does not occur to him that those who have
come to his defense against his detractor have a right
to ask what methods he had employed when in power,
and how he had dealt with those who did not sub-
scribe to his dictum as gospel truth. . . .

". . . Leon Trotsky will have it that criticism of
his past in the Kronstadt tragedy is only to aid and
abet his mortal enemy, Stalin. It does not occur to him
that one might detest the savage in the Kremlin and
his cruel regime and yet not exonerate Leon Trotsky
from the crime against the sailors of Kronstadt. In
point of truth I see no marked difference between the
two protagonists of the benevolent system of the dic-

tatorship except that Leon Trotsky is no longer in power to enforce its blessings, and Joseph Stalin is. I must, however, point out that Stalin did not come down as a gift from heaven to the hapless Russian people. He is merely continuing the Bolshevik traditions, even if in a more relentless manner.

". . . I admit, the dictatorship under Stalin's rule has become monstrous. That does not, however, lessen the guilt of Leon Trotsky as one of the actors in the revolutionary drama of which Kronstadt was one of the bloodiest scenes."

This is Emma Goldman, taking Trotsky to task for his role in the Kronstadt Rebellion in her pamphlet "Trotsky Protests Too Much," 1938.

What particularly incensed Emma Goldman was that Trotsky in exile, defending the purity of his revolutionary activities, tried to besmirch the Kronstadt sailors, representing them as riff-raff who had forgotten the revolutionary traditions of the original Kronstadt sailors, accusing them of being speculators in cloth, coal and bread. In 1919, when conditions were critical in hungry Petrograd, Trotsky declared, the Politbureau more than once discussed the possibility of securing an internal loan from Kronstadt (which had a quantity of old provisions), but the delegates of the Petrograd workers said that it was impossible to obtain anything from the Kronstadt sailors by kindness. In justification for the punishment meted out to Kronstadt, Trotsky repeated the claims of the Bolsheviks that "nearly all the old sailors who had taken part in the October Revolution were at the front, heroically fighting in the ranks of the Red Army. The naval replenishments consisted of new men, who had not been schooled in the revolution. These were a per-

fectly raw peasant mass who gave expression to the peasantry's discontent with the surplus-appropriation system."[42]
The Bolshevik conclusion was:

"This enabled the Socialist-Revolutionaries, Mensheviks and Whiteguards to worm their way into Kronstadt and to seize control of it."[43]

But the accusation somehow does not coincide with the fact that these same "speculators" and "riff-raff" were siding with the hungry proletariat of Petrograd, demanding that the workers be given equal rations with the privileged Communists.

The physical presence of Socialist-Revolutionaries, Mensheviks and Whiteguards in Kronstadt at that time, or of people who sympathized with other than the Communist party, is difficult to confirm or deny. Only in 1921 did the Communists inaugurate their campaign of complete extermination of other parties. We are willing to assume that Socialist-Revolutionaries, Mensheviks or people in sympathy with their programs (particularly with the land-reforms of the SR's), lived in Kronstadt and even influenced the editing of the historic 15-point resolution of the crews of the First and Second Squadrons of the Baltic Fleet (March 1st, 1921.)

From the Communist viewpoint, the resolution in itself was a crime punishable by death, and thousands of Kronstadters were liquidated for subscribing to it. By any civilized standards, the resolution reflected the desperate plight of a suffering people, who demanded that injustices be removed and freedom be restored.

As for the "Whiteguards," even if any were in the fortress city during the rebellion, it was hardly possibly for them to identify themselves or become vocal in view of the general revolutionary spirit of the Kronstadt sailors, soldiers and workers.

"Far from having anything to do with generals and counter-revolutionists, the Kronstadt sailors refused to accept aid even from the Socialist-Revolutionist Party. Its leader, Victor Tchernov, then in Reval, attempted to influence the sailors in favor of his party and its demands, but received no encouragement from The Provisional Revolutionary Committee. Chernov sent to Kronstadt the following radio-message:

" 'The Chairman of the Constitutional Assembly, Victor Tchernov, sends his fraternal greetings to the heroic comrades-sailors, the Red Army men and workers, who for the third time since 1905 are throwing off the yoke of tyranny. He offers to aid with men and to provision Kronstadt through the Russian cooperatives abroad. Inform what and how much is needed. Am prepared to come in person and give my energies and authority to the service of the people's revolution. I have faith in the final victory of the laboring masses . . . Hail to the first to raise the banner of the people's liberation! Down with despotism from left and right!' "[44]

The Kronstadt Revolutionary Committee declined the offers of the Socialist-Revolutionist Party and its leader Tchernov. It sent the following reply to Victor Tchernov:

"The Provisional Revolutionary Committee of Kronstadt expresses to all brothers abroad its deep gratitude for their sympathy. The Provisional Revolutionary Committee is thankful for the offer of

Comrade Tchernov, but it refrains for the present; that is, till further developments become clarified. Meanwhile everything will be taken into consideration.

> PETRICHENKO
> Chairman, Provisional
> Revolutionary Committee"[45]

The fact remains that the Kronstadt sailors did not accept any outside help, which proved one of their many tragic mistakes. They relied upon their own inadequate resources. If the Rebellion had been successful, they might have turned to the Socialist-Revolutionary Party for political leadership. This we may assume from the mental reservations indicated in the reply that the Chairman, Petrichenko, of the Provisional Committee, made to Victor Chernov. No doubt the Communists were aware of this. An assumption, however, is not a fact. But to Communists it has the same validity, and on the basis of this "fact," they put together their story that the discontent of the Kronstadt sailors "enabled the Socialist-Revolutionaries, Mensheviks and Whiteguards to worm their way into Kronstadt and to SEIZE CONTROL OF IT."

In the naked fight to maintain its power, the Communist Party could tolerate no opposition. The Kronstadt rebellion, from the Bolshevik point of view, was a great plot "designed" by their enemies—inside and outside Russia—to embarrass them at the moment when they were preparing to establish business and diplomatic relations with other countries. Characteristic of their campaign of misrepresentation and in order to justify the later butchery of the Kronstadt sailors, the Bolsheviks sent out the following radio broadcast at the beginning of March, 1921:

Bolsh looked upon Kron uprising as an embarr situation

". . . Just at this moment, when in America a new
republican regime is assuming the reins of government
and *SHOWING INCLINATIONS TO TAKE UP
BUSINESS RELATIONS WITH SOVIET RUS-
SIA* (our emphasis, E.P.), the spreading of lying
rumors and the organization of disturbances in Kronstadt have the sole purpose of influencing the new
American President in changing his policy toward
Russia. At the same time the London Conference is
holding its sessions, and the spreading of similar
rumors must influence also the Turkish delegation and
make it more submissive to the demands of the Entente. The rebellion of the *Petropavlovsk* crew is un-
doubtedly part of a great conspiracy to create trouble
within Soviet Russia and to injure our international
position. . . . This plan is being carried out within
Russia by a Tsarist general and former officers, and
their activities are supported by the Mensheviki and
Socialist-Revolutionists."[46]

To claim that the spontaneous revolt in Kronstadt was
designed to influence American policy toward the Soviet
Union was utterly ridiculous. A casual glance at American
newspapers of that period would suffice to prove how far
America was from any thought of recognizing Russia. On
the contrary, America believed that, in spite of apparent
victories in the civil war, the Communist regime would fall
victim to its own consuming fire. It took twelve more years
of subtle Soviet propaganda, an American depression, and a
new American president to provide the necessary climate
for United States' recognition of the Soviet regime.

One is overcome by a feeling of weariness when he takes
upon himself the task of chasing the swarm of misrepresenta-

tions, half truths and outright lies generously strewn in every piece of Communist "historical" work. A hundred new lies replace every one proved false. It appears to be deliberate Communist policy to drown each fresh issue as it arises in a flood of misrepresentations and refined twists, to becloud the truth in all matters. Communist "truth" must be tailored to fit the occasion. The Bolsheviks never wanted the real truth about Kronstadt—for it was one of the most shameful pages of Soviet history. To attempt to bury it was the proper course for the Communists. Even with the aid of passing time, however, they could not obliterate the memory of the grim events in the fortress city thirty-eight years ago.

X

TO SUM UP

The Kronstadt mutiny was preceded by several peasant revolts in different parts of Russia. The peasants conducted a fierce partisan warfare against Government forces, resisting food requisitions and other measures. In August, 1920, the major peasant uprising of that period (associated with the peasant leader, Antonov) occurred in Tambov Province.

The Communists read well these ominous signs of the time, understood them, and met them with the usual policy of dispatching punitive expeditions of Cheka and kursanti to the affected regions. Hostages were shot, homes of those peasants who fought in the ranks of the partisans were demolished or burned.

This situation might well have continued for a long time were it not for the unexpected and far more serious mutiny of the Kronstadt sailors. Kronstadt had been the stronghold of Bolshevism since 1917. Disaffection of the loyal guards, of the "pride of the Revolution," could not be ignored as were the peasants' demands. The Government was shocked into re-examining and altering its economic program for the sake of its very survival. The New Economic Policy was the solution—but not until the rebellion had been put down and the intransigent sailors punished.

The sailors of Kronstadt, an independent, spirited lot, hated privilege and authority. Cognizant of their role in the Revolution, they felt entitled to participate in the affairs of the State they helped to create. They, the armed knights of the Revolution, had a protective attitude toward the Petrograd workers who were the first to bear the burdens of the Revolution. Consequently, Kronstadt watched apprehensively the workers forced to strike at nearby Petrograd for food rations, equal distribution of food, and the abolition of privileges to Communists. What was the Government's answer? Armed kursanti (the students of the Soviet military schools) who dispersed the workers gathered at the factory gates and fired upon them, and enforced an 11 p.m. curfew. This official tyranny roused the Kronstadt garrison to frenzy.

We know that crews of the First and Second Squadrons of the Baltic Fleet (meeting in Yakorny Square in Kronstadt March 1st, 1921) then issued the famous 15-point resolution and that the Bolsheviks, disregarding these demands, sent Kronstadt an ultimatum to submit or be destroyed. On March 7, 1921, at 6:45 p.m., the Government unleashed its attack against the fortress.

In their actions, the Kronstadters were inspired by love of a free Russia. They were confident (mistakenly) of gaining the support of the whole of Russia, particularly of Petrograd, thus bringing about the country's liberation. They felt that they truly expressed the will of the people yearning for freedom and the opportunity to shape their own destinies.

On March 15th, two days before Kronstadt was subdued, Lenin declared at the 10th Assembly of the Communist

Party that the dissatisfaction of the peasantry, whose will had been definitely expressed, had to be reckoned with. Pointing out that the Socialist revolution, which had not yet advanced into other countries, could be saved only by agreement with the peasantry, he urged reconsideration of the policy toward them. Lenin realized that economically it would be impossible for the Communists to stay in power while waging war with the peasant. He realized, too, that the crisis was also of a political nature, and that it menaced the very existence of Communist rule. He had already decided upon a change in economic policy. But he was determined not to concede an inch in reference to the Bolshevik principle: absolute dictatorship of the Communist Party. Therefore, the Government used Kronstadt as an example to the rest of the country to prove once and for all that it would not tolerate having an issue forced from below; that its power must never be challenged; that a relaxation of its grip, if any, must come from above—another familiar characteristic of the despot's psychological make-up.

At the Communist Party Congress, the entire Bolshevik economic policy was changed as a result of the Kronstadt Rebellion and uprisings in other parts of the country. The Bolsheviks preferred to reverse their basic economic policies, to abolish the food requisitions, introduce a semblance of trade, grant concessions to capitalists—in short, give up Communism, for which the October Revolution presumably had been fought—rather than permit freely elected Soviets. Here lies the crux of the whole problem. The Communists would go to any length to preserve their power.

Lenin never made a secret of his aims, and his cynical attitude towards the methods of gaining and holding power is a matter of record. Indeed, among the first lessons taught a Communist is how to acquire and maintain power. In October, 1917, on the eve of the Bolshevik coup d'etat, Lenin asked the question, "Will the Bolsheviks be able to retain power?" His answer was: "The State is an organ or machine for the domination of one class over the others. One hundred and thirty thousand landlords have been able to rule over Russia. Cannot 240,000 members of the Bolshevik Party now do the same?" What the Bolsheviks wanted at first, Lenin argued, was the support of SOME sections of the population, the PASSIVE attitude of others and the INDECISION of the great majority. The discontented elements could and should be forcibly suppressed. Here is a simple recipe for seizing power, which the Communists have adhered to ever since.

It should be clear by now that all the prattle about the Communist State being a Workers' and Peasants' State is a myth, particularly cultivated abroad. The Russian people know better. Within Russia, the Communists do not even pretend any more. *They* know and the people know that the Communist Party is the absolute ruler of the country and its will is supreme; that the greatest police-system ever created by any government insures that the spirit of the people is kept, according to the Russian saying, "quieter than the water, lower than grass."

Russia at present is the most "peaceful" country in the world—with the peace and quiet of the cemetery. The Bolsheviks required forty years to establish their "peace," to weed out every vestige of independent thought and action. Only in the prisons and concentration camps does freedom of thought and expression exist. Occasionally, through a lucky escapee from behind the Iron Curtain, we can hear the anguished, despairing voice of the Russian people. It is a lonely voice crying in the dark of night in the cemetery which is Russia today, crying among the tomb-stones for buried freedoms. There, too, lie the sailors of Kronstadt, the victims of the first great challenge to the Communists' despotic regime.

Those Kronstadt heroes made the first great effort in Russia to throw off the yoke of the Communist order. It was actually an heroic attempt to start a Third Revolution. The attempt was unsuccessful. But despite all efforts of the present-day Soviet leaders to obtain from the Western world its blessing for a status quo in the Communist realm, a revolutionary change in Russia must yet take place if we have any faith in the everlasting, all-conquering spirit of free men.

REFERENCES

1. George Vernadsky, *A History of Russia.* Yale University Press (1944) p. 291.
2. Emma Goldman, *The Crushing of the Russian Revolution* (Freedom Press, London, 1922) p. 13.
3. S. P. Melgunov, *The Red Terror in Russia* (Berlin, 1924) pp. 120-22. (In Russian)
4. Emma Goldman, *Living My Life* (Alfred A. Knopf, Inc., 1931) p. 872.
5. Alexander Berkman, "The Kronstadt Rebellion," *Russian Revolution Series*, No. 3, (1922) pp. 9-11.
6. Emma Goldman, *Living My Life* (1931) p. 878.
7. *Ibid.*, p. 879.
8. *Ibid.*, pp. 880-881.
9. Alexander Berkman, op. cit., p. 13.
10. *Ibid.*, p. 13.
11. *Ibid.*, p. 15.
12. *Ibid.*, pp. 16-17.
13, 14, 15, 16. *Ibid.*, p. 18.
17, 18. *Ibid.*, p. 19.
19. *Ibid.*, pp. 23-24.
20. *Ibid.*, pp. 26, 28.
21. *Ibid.*, pp. 29-30.

22. See Trotsky's Order in Appendix, IV.
23. Alexander Berkman, *op. cit.*, p. 32.
24. Emma Goldman, *Living My Life* (1931), pp. 886-887.
25. *Ibid.*, p. 884.
26. *Ibid.*, p. 883.
27. Alexander Berkman, *op. cit.*, pp. 34-35.
28. *Ibid.*, p. 34.
29. *Ibid.*, pp. 24-25.
30. *Ibid.*, p. 40.
31. *Ibid.*, p. 36.
32. *Ibid.*, pp. 36-37.
33. Eugene Lyons, *Our Secret Allies* (1953), p. 126.
34. S. P. Melgunov, *op. cit.*, p. 21.
35. *The Truth About Kronstadt.* Prague, 1921. (In Russian) Published by the Russian newspaper "Volia Rossiyi" (Freedom of Russia)
35a. Alexander Berkman, *op. cit.*, p. 39.
36. Emma Goldman, *Living My Life* (1931) pp. 886-887.
37. See Appendix, II.
38. Nicholas Makeev & Valentine O'Hara, *Russia* (1925), p. 258.
38a. *Ibid.*, pp. 261-262.
39. *Ibid.*, p. 262.
40. *Ibid.*, p. 262.
41. *Ibid.*, p. 262.
42. *History of the Communist Party of the Soviet Union,* International Publishers (1939) p. 250.
43. *Ibid.*, p. 250.
44, 45. Alexander Berkman, *op. cit.*, pp. 15-16.
46. *Ibid.*, p. 17.

APPENDIX

I.

"The Kronstadt mutiny, which took place March 2-17, 1921, among the sailors of the forts and ships stationed in Kronstadt, was prepared by foreign and native counter-revolutionaries who made use of the dissatisfaction affecting some layers of the peasant population because of the drain upon the country resulting from four years of imperialist and three years of civil war.

"It is absolutely clear that here was the work of the SR's [members of the Socialist-Revolutionaries' party] and of the Whiteguards abroad; it was a movement which boiled down to a petty-bourgeois anarchic upheaval. . . . We met with the petty-bourgeois anarchic elements in the Russian revolution, we fought them during tens of years. . . . They all came with the slogans of equality, freedom, constitutional assembly, and more than once turned out to be a treadle, a bridge to the next step of Whiteguard power." (Lenin, *Works*, Vol. XXVI, pp. 214-215.)

II.

"A definite role in the development of anti-Soviet agitation among the sailors and in tearing them away from the party was played by the factional struggle carried on by the Trotskyites and Bukharinites, a struggle that went on during the discussions over the role of the trade-unions at the end of 1920 and the beginning of 1921. Preparation of the mutiny was carried on long before it took place. The counter-revolutionary press abroad raised a campaign of lies about the situation in the country. Seventeen days before the start of the mutiny, the Paris press carried news that a mutiny had broken out in Kronstadt.

"The change in the social complexion of the Kronstadt garrison contributed to the momentary success of the counter-revolution. By that time, the best elements of the Baltic Fleet had left for the fronts, and the command of the Fleet strenuously recruited as replacements those elements least stable politically. The composition of the new recruitments into the Fleet consisted partially of declassed elements among whom the SR's, the Mensheviks and Anarchists carried on their counter-revolutionary agitation to the fullest extent.

"Trotsky and Zinoviev, who subsequently found themselves in the camp of counter-revolution and among the German-Japanese spies and diversionists, having advance information about the preparation of the mutiny, concealed this from the party and government; when the mutiny started they failed to take immediately the necessary resolute steps for its suppression.

"Upon the return of the delegates sent to Petrograd for anti-Soviet agitation among the workers, the organizers of the mutiny spread false rumors about an uprising in Petrograd, and at a meeting on the battleships pushed through an SR-resolution whose basic theses were exactly in line with the statements of the platform of the Trotsky-Bukharin opposition.

"M. I. Kalinin appeared March 1st at the meeting attended by many thousands in Kronstadt. After Comrade

Kalinin's departure, the organizers of the mutiny introduced slogans such as "free trade," "free Soviets," etc., attempting thereby to create dissatisfaction among the masses with the Soviet power, masking their activity with the slogan: 'For the Soviets, but without the Communists.'

"March 2nd, the organizers of the mutiny arrested the Commissar of the Fleet, N. Kuzmin, and others; and officially created a "Revkom" (Revolutionary Committee) headed by the SR, Petrichenko. Through Finland connections were established with foreign interventionists and White Guards abroad. A staff was organized, headed by General Koslovsky,

"The situation was extraordinarily complicated by the fact that the ice had begun to thaw; if the ice in the bay broke up it would cut off Kronstadt from Petrograd, thus excluding land operations against Kronstadt, where all the ships of the Baltic Fleet were stationed. Relying upon this Fleet and the impregnability of Kronstadt, the imperialists could directly menace Petrograd and start a new campaign against the Soviet land. It was necessary to liquidate the mutiny as soon as possible. Since the mutineers refused to surrender, it was decided to begin the assault upon Kronstadt.

"The arrival of 300 delegates of the Tenth Congress of the Party, headed by Comrade Voroshilov, played a decisive role in the suppression of the mutiny. Upon joining the army units, they carried through the basic work of raising the fighting capacities of the units and strengthening their confidence in victory.

"Comrade Voroshilov, who headed the units as a member of the Revolutionary Military Council of the decisive Southern Grouping, did a great job in devising the most expedient measures for the organization of the attack and in working out the operation plan of action against the mutineers.

"The forces of the mutineers reached the mark of 10,000 men; they had at their disposal 68 machine-guns and 135 field-guns.

"The open approaches over the ice-fields greatly complicated the organization of the attack. Preparations for storming the sea fortress were begun.

"The first attack on March 8th pointed up the necessity of increasing the contingents and the fighting power and the need for special tactical preparation of the troops for successful action in the unique circumstances of open ice-fields. To aid the fighting troops, new units were called out, also air-force and artillery.

"On March 16th an increased bombardment of Kronstadt and its forts was begun and the air-force went into action.

"During the night of March 17th, an attack on the ice of the Finnish Bay was undertaken by two groupings of troops from Oranienbaum and Sestroretsk. The troops, in white capes, moved toward Kronstadt under cover of night over the ice which begun to thaw in places. The projectors of the mutineers illuminated the ice-fields in attempts to locate the attacking force. Overcoming the surge of fire from machine-guns and field-pieces and the obstacles of barbed wire, the red troops of the Southern Grouping reached Kronstadt at dawn and in a violent attack rushed the city.

"March 17th saw bitter fighting on the streets of Kronstadt. Comrade Voroshilov led the Red troops directly in this battle.

"The kursanti (students of military academies) simultaneously led the attack upon the Northern forts of Kronstadt.

"Bursting into the city on the night of March 18th, the heroic kursanti captured the staff headquarters of the fortress.

The crews of the battleships *Petropavlovsk* and *Sevastopol*, who had arrested their leaders, surrendered. The leaders and some other mutineers escaped to Finland.

"On March 18th Kronstadt again became Soviet.

"At first, the emigres abroad greeted the Kronstadt mutiny with a joyous howl. The capitalists, the kadets (Constitutional Democrats), the SR's headed by Victor Chernov (who had taken the occasion to come to Reval) were making lavish preparations to aid the mutineers with food. Miliukov, aware of the political situation and counting upon a further development of the petty-bourgeois counter-revolution, brought forward the speculative slogan, "Soviets without Communists." However, the disturbances which took place in the spring of 1921, after the Kronstadt mutiny, petered out through the liquidation of the Antonov uprising and the individual bandit-gangs in the Ukraine.

"The Lenin policy of the NEP deprived the counter-revolutionists of any ground for agitation in the villages, and under the leadership of the proletariat strengthened the unity of the working-class and the peasantry."

Translated from:
(*Bolshaia Sovietskaia Enciclopedia*. Gosudarstvenny Institut, tome 35. Moskva, Ogiz. RSFSR. 1937. stranitzi 222-223—The Large Soviet Encyclopedia, Vol. 35. Moscow. Ogiz. RSFSR. 1937. pp. 222-223.)

III.

THE KRONSTADT MUTINY

"Kronstadt mutiny—a counter-revolutionary mutiny against the Soviet power, which took place in 1921, from

February 28 to March 18, inclusive. Heading the mutiny were Whiteguards, who had connections with the SR's (Socialist-Revolutionaries), Mensheviks and representatives of foreign states.

"At first the mutineers tried to cover their aspirations to restore the power and properties of the capitalists and landowners with a 'Soviet' sign-board. They brought forth the slogan: 'Soviets without Communists.' Counter-revolutionaries attempted to utilize the petty-bourgeois masses' dissatisfaction with war-communism, in order to overthrow the Soviet power. The enemies of the Soviets took advantage of the following factors: the Kronstadt Bolshevik organization had been weakened through mobilization of its members for the Front; the leading group of the revolutionary sailors of the Baltic Fleet were fighting on different fronts of the Civil War; and Trotsky proteges were sending captured Makhno* followers into the fleet for purposes of diversion. This provided them with the opportunity to seize the best fortress of the Soviet Republic. Three hundred delegates of the 10th Congress of the Communist Party, which was then in session, under the leadership of Voroshilov, were sent into the Red Army units taking part in the liquidation of the mutiny. On March 18, 1921, through an heroic assault upon Kronstadt on the ice of the Finnish Bay, the mutiny was crushed."

---

* Makhno movement.

A counter-revolutionary movement of middle-income peasants (kulaks) in the Ukraine during the years of the Civil War in Russia. At the head of one of the larger kulak-bands stood Makhno, who declared himself an Anarchist. His base of operation was the village Guliai-Polie in the region of Yekaterinoslav in the Ukraine. The Makhno movement was "liquidated" (Soviet term for *disposing of.* E. P.) by punitive expeditions headed by Comrades Frunze, Voroshilov, Budenny. In 1921 Makhno escaped to Rumania. He died in Paris in 1934.

(*Politicheski Slovar.* Gosudarstvennoye Izdatelstvo Politicheskoy Literaturi. 1940. Stranitza 336—*Political Dictionary.* State Publishing House of Political Literature. 1940. p. 336.)

Translated from:
(*Politichesky Slovar*. Pod redaktsiay Alekhandrova, Galyianova, Rubinsteina. Gosudarstvennoie Izdatelstvo Politicheskoi Literaturi. 1940. Stranitzi 294-5.—*Soviet Political Dictionary*. State Publishing House of Political Literature. 1940. pp. 294-5.)

IV.

". . . The Party was confronted with the necessity of working out a new line of policy on all questions affecting the economics of the country, a line that would meet the new situation.

"And the Party proceeded to work out such a line of policy of questions of economic development.

"But the class enemy was not dozing. He tried to exploit the distressing economic situation and the discontent of the peasants for his own purposes. Kulak revolts, engineered by White-guards and Socialist-Revolutionaries, broke out in Siberia, the Ukraine and the Tambov province (Antonov's rebellion). All kinds of counter-revolutionaries, Anarchists, Whiteguards, bourgeois nationalists became active again. The enemy adopted new tactics of struggle against the Soviet power. He began to borrow a Soviet garb, and his slogan was no longer the old bankrupt 'Down with the Soviets!' but a new slogan: 'For the Soviets, but without Communists!'

"A glaring instance of the new tactics of the class enemy was the counter-revolutionary mutiny in Kronstadt. It began in March, 1921, a week before the Tenth Party Congress. Whiteguards, in complicity with Socialist-Revolutionaries, Mensheviks and representatives of foreign states, assumed the lead of the mutiny. The mutineers at first used a 'Soviet' sign-board to camouflage their purpose of restoring the power and property of the capitalists and landlords. They raised the cry: 'Soviets without Communists!' The counter-revolutionaries tried to exploit the discontent of the petty bourgeois masses in order to overthrow the power of the Soviets under a pseudo-Soviet slogan.

"Two circumstances facilitated the outbreak of the Kronstadt mutiny: the deterioration in the composition of the ships' crews, and weakness of the Bolshevik organization in Kronstadt. Nearly all the old sailors who had taken part in the October Revolution were at the front, heroically fighting in the ranks of the Red Army. The naval replenishments consisted of new men, who had not been schooled in the revolution. These were a perfectly raw peasant mass who gave expression to the peasantry's discontent with the surplus-appropriation system. As for the Bolshevik organization in Kronstadt, it had been greatly weakened by a series of mobilizations for the front. This enabled the Socialist-Revolutionaries, Mensheviks and Whiteguards to worm their way into Kronstadt and to seize control of it.

"The mutineers gained possession of a first-class fortress, the fleet, and a vast quantity of arms and ammunition. The international counter-revolutionaries were triumphant. But their jubilation was premature. The mutiny was quickly put down by Soviet troops. Against the Kronstadt mutineers the Party sent its finest sons—delegates to the Tenth Congress, headed by Comrade Voroshilov. The Red Army men advanced on Kronstadt across a thin sheet of ice; it broke in places and many were drowned. The almost impregnable forts of Kronstadt had to be taken by storm; but loyalty to the revolution, bravery and readiness to die for the Soviets won the day. The fortress of Kronstadt fell before the onslaught of the Red troops. The Kronstadt mutiny was suppressed."

"History of the Communist Party of the Soviet Union. (Bolshevik). International Publishers, New York (1939). pp. 249-250.

V.

ULTIMATUM TO KRONSTADT

"The Workers' and Peasants' Government has decreed that Kronstadt and the rebellious ships must immediately submit to the authority of the Soviet Republic. Therefore I command all who have raised their hand against the Socialist fatherland to lay down their arms at once. The obdurate are to be disarmed and turned over to the Soviet authorities. The arrested Commissars and other representatives of the Government are to be liberated at once. Only those surrendering unconditionally may count on the mercy of the Soviet Republic.

"Simultaneously I am issuing orders to prepare to quell the mutiny and subdue the mutineers by force of arms. Responsibility for the harm that may be suffered by the peaceful population will fall entirely upon the heads of the counter-revolutionary mutineers. This warning is final.

> TROTSKY
> Chairman, Revolutionary
> Military Soviet of the
> Republic
> KAMENEV
> Commander-in-Chief"

("The Kronstadt Rebellion," Alexander Berkman. *Russian Revolutionary Series*, No. 3. Berlin, 1922.)

VI.

ABUSE OF THE WHITE FLAG

"A white flag hoisted during a field battle means a temporary halt in war activities between enemies. That's the way it always was among peoples.

"But not with the Communists. They turn the flag of peace into a tool of betrayal and under its cover commit acts of atrocity.

"Yesterday, March 8th, a group of Red Army soldiers carrying a white flag left Oranienbaum and went in the direction of Kronstadt. Seeing these approaching emissaries, two of our men on horseback went to meet the delegation unarmed. One of our men approached the enemy group closely, but the other stopped at a short distance away. Before our first man had a chance to say a few words, he was pounced upon by the Communists, dragged from the horse, and carried off. Our second man immediately turned around and rushed back to the fortress.

"This is an episode worth everybody's attention, showing the methods used by the Communists against the working masses."

(*Izvestia* of the Provisional Revolutionary Committee of Sailors, Red Army Men and Workers of the City of Kronstadt. Wednesday, March 9th, 1921. Issue No. 7). *Note:* The *Izvestia* was published daily during the 18-day period of the Kronstadt rebellion.

BIBLIOGRAPHY

Barmine, Alexander, *One Who Survived*, (Putnam, 1945)

Berkman, Alexander, "The Kronstadt Rebellion" (pamphlet), *Russian Revolution Series*. (Berlin, 1922)

Carr, Edward Hallett, *The Bolshevik Revolution, 1917-1923*. I. (Macmillan Co., 1952)

Chamberlin, William Henry, *The Russian Enigma* (Scribner's, 1943)

Ciliga, Anton, *The Kronstadt Revolt* (Freedom Press, London, 1942)

Goldman, Emma, *The Crushing of the Russian Revolution* (Freedom Press, London, 1922)

Goldman, Emma, *My Further Disillusionment in Russia* (Doubleday, 1924)

Goldman, Emma, *Living My Life* (Alfred A. Knopf, Inc., New York, 1931)

Goldman, Emma, "Trotsky Protests Too Much" (pamphlet) (Anarchist-Communist Federation, Glasgow, 1938)

History of the Communist Party of the Soviet Union, International Publishers. (New York, 1939) (Bolshevik)

Lyons, Eugene, *Our Secret Allies* (Duell, Sloan & Pearce, New York, 1953)

Makeev, Nicholas & O'Hara, Valentine, *Russia* (Scribner's, 1943, and Ernest Benn Ltd., London, 1925)

Melgunov, S. P., *The Red Terror In Russia* (in Russian), (Berlin, 1924)

Pankratova, Prof. A. M., *History of the USSR* (in Russian), (Uchpedgiz, 1948)

Pares, Sir Bernard, *A History of Russia* (Alfred A. Knopf, 1948)

Politichesky Slovar, Gosudarstvennoie Izdatelstvo Politicheskoy Liteartury. 1940. (Political Dictionary. State Publishing House of Political Literature) (in Russian)

Rothstein, Andrew, *A History of the USSR* (Pelican, 1950)

Shub, David, *Lenin*, (Mentor Books, 1948)

Spargo, John, *Bolshevism, the Enemy of Political and Industrial Democracy* (Harper & Bros., 1919)

Cheka, Central Bureau of the Socialist-Revolutionary Party, (Research in the activities of the Extraordinary Commissions) (Berlin, 1922) (in Russian)

Vernadsky, George, *A. History of Russia* (Yale University Press, 1944)

Bolshaia Sovietskaia Enciclopedia, Gosudarstvenny Institut. Ogiz. RSFSR. Moskva. (1937)

(*The Large Soviet Encyclopoedia*, State Institute "Soviet Encyclopoedia." Ogiz. Moscow, RSFSR. Vol. 35.)

INDEX